S0-CCY-476

To IAN:

Thanks for stopping
by!
Remember to laugh
out loud!

Billie :)

Book #1

A

COLLECTION

OF

E-MAILS

Billie Jo Mouren
and
Gwen Andersen

A COLLECTION OF EMAILS - BOOK #1

Co-Authors: Billie Jo Mouren and Gwen Andersen
Cover and Interior Design: Billie Jo Mouren
Editor: Gwen Andersen
Email Address: info@ ˙˙˙˙˙˙˙ s.com
Wet ˙˙˙˙˙˙˙ s.com

TO ORDER MORE BOOKS:
Telephone Billie Jo: (949) 500-5272
Email Billie Jo: belejo7@gmail.com
P. O.] Payment: Cash or check ˙˙˙˙˙9-2677

Printed in the U.S.A.
A Collection of Emails - Book #1 is a registered Copyright
All rights reserved.   First Edition: 2007
Library of Congress Control Number: 2007908363
ISBN: 978-0-9801222-0-6 for
A COLLECTION OF EMAILS - BOOK #1

FOR BULK DISCOUNT ORDERS: Please contact Funny Books, LLC
at: info@acollectionofemails.com or above address.

NO PART OF THIS PUBLICATION MAY BE REPRODUCED, stored in a retrieval system or transmitted in any form or by any means, electronic, mechanical photocopying, recording, scanning, or otherwise, except as permitted under Section 107 or 108 of the 1976 United States Copyright Act. Exceptions are made for brief excerpts used in published reviews. Some of the designations used by manufacturers and seller to distinguish their products are claimed as trademarks.

WARNINGS, LIMIT OF LIABILITY and DISCLAIMER OF WARRANTY: While the publisher and authors have used their best efforts in preparing this book, they make no representations or warranties and assume no responsibility with respect to the accuracy, errors, omissions or completeness of the contents of this book and, specifically disclaim any implied warranties. The information provided is on an 'as is' basis. This is a humor book.

The accuracy and completeness of the information provided herein and the opinions stated herein are not guaranteed or warranted to produce any particular results and the advice and strategies contained herein may not be suitable for every individual, neither the publisher nor the authors shall be liable for any loss of profit or any damages; including, but not limited to, special incidental, consequential or other damages. Further, publisher and authors do not have control over or assume any responsibility for third party content. **This is a humor book.** The names used in all email entries are invented names, except notable public figures who are the subject of satire. Any use of real names is accidental and coincidental. Specific content of email entries was not originated by the authors. The 'collection, graphic layout and annotations' are the original work of the authors.

NOTE: If you purchased this book without a cover you should be aware that this book is stolen property. It was reported as 'unsold and destroyed' to the publisher and neither the authors nor the publisher has received any payment for this 'stripped book'.

DEDICATION

We lovingly dedicate this book to 'OUR LITERARY BABY'. Without her constant support, her patience, her love and her sincere constructive criticism we would not have been able to complete our first literary masterpiece! We especially appreciate her close and watchful eye over each creative process. Her selflessness could not be matched by any person during the tireless hours of work. Her tolerance and understanding of early mornings, late nights, missed meals, lack of exercise or any consistency in routine are sincerely appreciated. We thank you and love you, Baby.

We, also, sincerely thank *all of our friends, families and acquaintances* who contributed their emails to our collection. Keep up the good work!

Finally, of course, we thank our parents, especially Doris, for inspiring us with humor. Love you. . .

Billie Jo and Gwen

B A B Y

A NOTE TO OUR READERS

Each and every item in this book was received as an email from friends or acquaintances with encouragement to pass such information on to others. The *original* source for the majority of emails is unknown and/or was not identified. There is no way to verify the authenticity of information received via emails. It would seem prudent to keep in mind that possibly 98-99% of the humorous information circulated on the internet via emails is not factual or true, although it often makes for amusing reading, which is our only objective. **This is a humor book.** Therefore, do not take any of these entries too seriously.

FOR EMAIL CONTRIBUTIONS: If you have **not** seen an email in Book #1 you consider humorous and would like printed, you may send your email contribution(s) **for Book #2** to: info@acollectionofemails.com. *Absolutely NO x-rated, excessively profane or seriously off-color material will be saved and sender(s) of such emails will be blocked.*

TABLE OF CONTENT

CHAPTER 1

(Okay, Billie Jo, let's get going! ga)

OLDER PEOPLE - SURPRISING PROBLEMS

Older people have problems that you haven't even considered yet! An 87 year old man, named Bill, was requested by his doctor a sperm count as part of his physical exam. The doctor gave Bill a jar and said, "Take this jar home and bring back a semen sample tomorrow." The next day, Bill reappeared at the doctor's office and gave him the jar, which was as clean and empty as the previous day. The doctor asked what happened. Bill explained, "Well, doc, it's like this. First I tried with my right hand, but nothing. Then I tried with my left hand, but still nothing. Then I asked my wife, Doris, for help. She tried with her right hand, then with her left, still nothing. She tried with her mouth, first with her teeth in, then with her teeth out, still nothing. We even called up Juanda, the lady next door, and she also tried. First with both hands, then an armpit and she even tried squeezin' it between her knees, but still nothing. The doctor was shocked! "You asked your neighbor?" The old man replied, *"Yep, none of us could get the dang jar open."*

PHOTOS - HOW TO GET A MAN TO WASH HIS HANDS

LIVING WILL

Last night my friend and I were sitting in the living room. I said to her, "I never want to live in a vegetative state, dependent on some machine and fluids from a bottle. If that ever happens, just pull the plug." She got up, unplugged the TV and threw out my wine.... She's such a bitch!

1

BLONDE - HUSBAND

A blonde guy gets home early from work and hears strange noises coming from the bedroom. He rushes upstairs to find his wife naked on the bed, sweating and panting. "What's wrong?" he says. "I'm having a heart attack," cries his wife. He rushes downstairs to grab the phone, but just as he's dialing, his 4 year old son comes up and says, "Daddy! Daddy! Uncle Ted is hiding in your closet and he's got no clothes on!" The guy slams the phone down and storms upstairs into the bedroom, past his screaming wife and rips open the wardrobe door. Sure enough, there is his brother, totally naked, cowering on the closet floor. "You rotten S.O.B." says the husband, "My wife is having a heart attack and you're running around naked scaring the kids!"

WOMAN'S PERFECT BREAKFAST

She's sitting at the table with her gourmet coffee.
Her son is on the cover of the Wheaties box.
Her daughter is on the cover of Business Week.
Her boyfriend is on the cover of Playgirl.
And her husband is on the back of the milk carton.

IRISH TOAST

John O'Reilly hoisted his beer and said, "Here's to spending the rest of me life between the legs of me wife!" This won him the top prize at the pub for the best toast of the night! He went home and told his wife, Mary, "I won the prize for the best toast of the night." She said, "Aye, did ye now. And what was your toast?" John said, "Here's to spending the rest of me life sitting in church beside me wife." "Oh, that is very nice indeed, John!" Mary said.

The next day Mary ran into one of John's drinking buddies on the street corner. The man chuckled leeringly and said, "John won the prize the other night at the pub with a toast about you, Mary." Mary said, "Aye, he told me and I was a bit surprised myself. You know, he's only been there twice in the last four years. Once he fell asleep and the other time I had to pull him by the ears to make him come!"

LETTER FROM WIFE

To my darling husband:

Before you return from your trip I just want to let you know about the small accident I had with the pickup truck when I turned into the driveway. Fortunately, it's not too bad and I really didn't get hurt, so please don't worry too much about me. I was coming home from Wal-Mart and when I turned into the driveway, I accidentally pushed down on the accelerator instead of the brakes. The garage door is slightly bent but the pickup, fortunately, came to a halt when it bumped into your car. I'm really sorry but I know with your kind-hearted personality you will forgive me. You know how much I love you and care for you, my sweetheart. I am enclosing a picture for you. I cannot wait to hold you in my arms again.

Your loving wife ...

P.S. YOUR GIRLFRIEND CALLED!

CIGARETTES and TAMPONS

Chris walks into a pharmacy and wanders up and down the aisles. The sales girl notices him and asks him if she can help him. Chris answers he is looking for a box of tampons for his wife, Cassidy. She directs him down the correct aisle. A few minutes later he deposits a huge bag of cotton balls and a ball of string on the counter. The clerk says, confused, "Sir, I thought you were looking for tampons for your wife?" He answers, "You see, it's like this. Yesterday I sent Cassidy to the store to get me a carton of cigarettes and she came back with a tin of tobacco and rolling papers... 'cause its *soooo* much cheaper'. So, I figure if I have to roll my own; so does she."

3

Nun BAR STOOL LEGS

Sisters Mary Catherine, Maria Theresa, Katherine Marie, Rose Frances and Mary Kathleen left the Convent on a trip to St. Patrick's Cathedral in New York City and were sight-seeing on a Tuesday in July. It was hot and humid in town and their traditional clothing was making them so uncomfortable, they decided to stop in at Patty McGuire's Pub for a cold soft drink.

Patty had recently added special legs to his barstools, which were the talk of the fashionable eastside neighborhood. All 5 Nuns sat up at the bar and were enjoying their refreshments when Monsignor Riley and Father McGinty entered the bar. They, too, were coming to enjoy a cool soft drink. Upon entering they were shocked and almost fainted at what they saw.

Dear Lord: Give us a sense of humor, Give us the grace to see a joke and pass it on to other people.

THE WEDDING INVITATION

YOU ARE REGRETFULLY INVITED
TO THE WEDDING BETWEEN MY PERFECT SON,

The Doctor

AND SOME

Cheap Two-Bit Tramp

WHOSE NAME ESCAPES ME RIGHT NOW.

THE BIGGEST DISASTER IN MY
FAMILY'S HISTORY WILL TAKE PLACE AT

9pm on Saturday, September 8th

AND NO DOUBT END IN DIVORCE.
HOPEFULLY IN TIME TO STILL BE ELIGIBLE FOR AN ANNULMENT.
THE OVERWHELMINGLY DISAPPOINTING HEARTBREAK OF A CEREMONY
WILL BE FOLLOWED BY DINNER, WHERE NUTS WILL BE SERVED
BECAUSE WHATSHERFACE HAS AN ALLERGY.

BLONDE - DOGS

A girl was visiting her blonde friend who had acquired two new dogs and asked what their names were. The blonde responded by saying, "One is named Rolex and the other one is named Timex." Her friend said, "Whoever heard of someone naming their dogs like that?" "Helloooo," answered the Blonde. "They're watch dogs!

THE WHY'S OF MEN . . .

1. Why do men become smarter during sex? Because they're plugged into a genius.

2. Why does it take 1M sperm to fertilize 1 egg? They don't stop to ask for directions.

3. Why don't women blink during sex? They don't have enough time.

4. Why do men snore when they lie on their back? Because their balls fall over their butt-hole and they vapor lock.

5. Why were men given larger brains than dogs? So they won't hump women's legs at cocktail parties.

6. Why did God make man before woman? He needed a rough draft before the masterpiece.

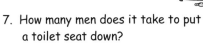

7. How many men does it take to put a toilet seat down? Don't know...it's never happened.

8. Why did God put men on earth? Because a vibrator can't mow the lawn.

9. What do you call an intelligent, good looking, sensitive guy? A rumor.

10. Why do little boys whine? They're practicing to be men.

11. What does it mean when a man is gasping for breath? You didn't hold the pillow down long enough.

12. How do you keep your husband from reading your emails? Rename your e-mail folder to Instruction Manual!

BLONDE - CAR

A blonde pushes her BMW into a gas station. She tells the mechanic it died. After he works on it for a few minutes it starts idling smoothly. She says, "What's the story?" He replies, "Just crap in the carburetor." She asks, "How often do I have to do that?"

TIDE

Dear Tide,

I am writing to say what an excellent product you have! I've used it all of my married life, as my Mom always told me it was the best. Now that I am in my fifties I find it even better! In fact, about a month ago, I  spilled some red wine on my new white blouse. My inconsiderate and uncaring husband started to belittle me about how clumsy I was and generally started becoming a pain in the neck. One thing led to another and somehow I ended up with his blood on my new white blouse!

I grabbed my bottle of Tide with bleach alternative and to my surprise and satisfaction all of the stains came out! In fact, the stains came out so well the detectives who came by yesterday told me that the DNA tests on my blouse were negative and then my attorney called and said that I was no longer considered a suspect in the disappearance of my husband. What a relief! Going through  menopause is bad enough without being a murder suspect.

I thank you once again for having a great product.

Well, gotta go, have to write to the Hefty bag people.

Hmmmmmmmm!!!

A husband and wife were sharing a  bottle of wine when the husband said, "I bet you can't tell me something that will make me feel happy and sad at the same time." The wife thought for a few moments, then said, "Your d**k's bigger than your brother's." Hmmmm....

QANTAS CHECKLIST - ABSOLUTELY HILARIOUS

After every flight, Qantas pilots fill out a form, called a 'gripe sheet', which tells mechanics about problems with the aircraft. The mechanics correct the problems; document their repairs on the form and then the pilots review the 'gripe sheets' before the next flight. Never let it be said that ground crews lack a sense of humor.

Here are some actual maintenance complaints submitted by Qantas **PILOTS** (marked with a **P**) and the **SOLUTION** recorded (marked with an **S**) by maintenance engineers:

P: Left inside main tire almost needs replacement
S: Almost replaced left inside main tire
P: Test flight OK, except auto-land very rough.
S: Auto-land not installed on this aircraft
P: Dead bugs on windshield
S: Live bugs on back-order
P: Autopilot in altitude-hold mode produces a 200 feet per minute descent
S: Cannot reproduce problem on ground
P: Something loose in cockpit
S: Something tightened in cockpit
P: Evidence of leak on right main landing gear
S: Evidence removed
P: DME volume unbelievably loud
S: DME volume set to more believable level
P: Friction locks cause throttle levers to stick
S: That's what friction locks are for
P: IFF inoperative in OFF mode
S: IFF always inoperative in OFF mode
P: Suspected crack in windshield
S: Suspect you're right
P: Number 3 engine missing
S: Engine found on right wing after brief search
P: Aircraft handles funny
S: Aircraft warned to straighten up, fly right, and be serious
P: Target radar hums
S: Reprogrammed target radar with lyrics
P: Mouse in cockpit
S: Cat installed
P: Noise coming from under instrument panel. Sounds like a midget pounding on something with a hammer
S: Took hammer away from midget

8

WIFE'S BOTTOM SIZE vs BBQ GRILL

A man and his wife were working in their garden one day and the man looks over at his wife and says, "Your butt is getting really big; I mean *really* big. I bet your butt is bigger than the barbecue grill." With that he proceeded to get a measuring tape and measure the grill and then went over to where his wife was working and measured his wife's bottom. "Yes, I was right; your butt is two inches wider than the barbeque grill!" The woman chose to ignore her husband. Later that night in bed, the husband is feeling frisky. He makes some advances toward his wife, who completely brushes him off. "What's wrong?" he asks. She answers, "Do you really think I'm going to fire up this Big-Ass grill for one little wiener?" Men are not equipped for this kind of contest!

PHOTOS - HAVE A NICE DAY!

BLONDE - KNITTING

A highway patrolman pulled alongside a speeding car on the freeway. Glancing at the car, he was astounded to see that the blonde behind the wheel, Karina, was knitting! Realizing that she was oblivious to his flashing lights and siren, the trooper cranked down his window, turned on his bullhorn and yelled, "PULL OVER!" "NO!" Karina yelled back, "IT'S A SCARF!"

9

REMEMBER - IDIOT

Never argue with idiots: they'll drag you down to their level and beat you with experience.

COMMENTS ABOUT MEN

- One day my housework-challenged husband decided to wash his sweat shirt. Seconds after entering the laundry room he shouted, "What setting do I use on the washing machine?" "It depends," I replied. "What does it say on your shirt?" He yelled back, "University of Oklahoma."
- A couple is lying in bed. The man says, "I am going to make you the happiest woman in the world." The woman replied, "I'll miss you..."
- "It's just too hot to wear clothes today," Jack says as he stepped out of the shower. "Honey, what do you think the neighbors would think if I mowed the lawn like this?" "Probably that I married you for your money," she replied.
- Dear Lord: I pray for Wisdom to understand my man; Love to forgive him; and Patience for his moods. Because, Lord, if I pray for Strength I'll beat him to death. AMEN

BLONDE - WAITRESS at TRUCK STOP

A trucker came into a truck stop cafe and placed his order. He said, "I want three flat tires, a pair of headlights and a pair of running boards." The brand new blonde waitress, Tina, not wanting to appear stupid, went to the kitchen and said to the cook, "This guy just ordered three flat tires, a pair of headlights and a pair of running boards. What does he think this place is? An auto parts store?" "No," the cook said. "Three flat tires means three pancakes, a pair of headlights is two eggs sunny side up and running boards are 2 slices of crisp bacon." "Oh, OK!" She said. Tina thought about it for a moment and then spooned up a bowl of beans and gave it to the customer. The trucker asked, "What are the beans for, Blondie?" Tina replied, "I thought while you were waiting for the flat tires, headlights and running boards you might as well gas up!" **(The blonde gets even)...**

SIGNS - SIGNS OF WHAT?

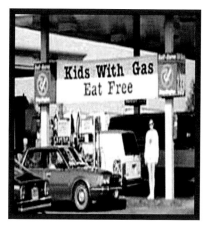

WHO DOES WHAT

A man and his wife were having an argument about who should brew the coffee each morning. The wife, Bobbie, said, "You should do it because you get up first and then we don't have to wait as long to get our coffee."   The husband, Eli, said, "You are in charge of cooking around here and you should do it because that's your job. I can just wait for my coffee." Bobbie replies, "No, you should do it and besides it's in the Bible that the man should do the coffee." Eli replies, "I can't believe that, show me." So Bobbie fetches the Bible, opens the New Testament and shows Eli at the top of several pages that it indeed says: 'HE BREWS'.

THE REDHEAD

A man is dining in a fancy restaurant and there is a gorgeous redhead sitting at the next table. He has been checking her out since he sat down, but lacks the nerve to talk to her. Suddenly, she sneezes and her glass eye came flying out of its socket toward the man. He spontaneously reaches out, grabs the glass eye out of the air and hands it back to her. "Oh, my, I am so sorry," the woman says as she pops her eye back in place. She says, "I'm sure that must have  embarrassed you so let me pay for your dinner to make it up to you." They enjoy a wonderful dinner together and afterwards they go to the theater followed by drinks. They talk, they laugh, she shares her deepest dreams and he listens and shares. After paying for everything, she asks him if he would like to come to her place for a nightcap and breakfast. They have a wonderful time. The next morning she cooks a gourmet breakfast with all the trimmings. The guy is amazed and totally impressed. Everything had been so incredible! "You know," he says, "You are the perfect woman. Are you this nice to every guy you meet?" "No," she replies, "you just happened to catch my eye!"

A NEW DRINK

A man walks into a bar, sits down and asks, "Bartender, got any specials today?" Bartender answers, "Yes, as a matter of fact, we have a new drink invented by a gynecologist patron of ours. It's a mix of Pabst Blue Ribbon beer and Smirnoff Vodka. The man asks, "Good grief, what do you call that?" The bartender replied, ***"It's a 'PABST SMIR'"***.

Her job is to Bitch...
Mine is to give her a reason!

Wipe your mouth, there's still a tiny bit of bullshit around your lips.

MAXINE - MEN

- How many men does it take to open a beer? None. It should be open when she brings it.
- Why is a Laundromat a really bad place to pick up a woman? Because a woman who can't afford a washing machine will probably never be able to support you.
- Why do women have smaller feet than men? It's one of those 'evolutionary things' that allows them to stand closer to the kitchen sink.
- How do you know when a woman is about to say something smart? When she starts a sentence with, "A man once told me…"
- How do you fix a woman's watch? You don't. There is a clock on the oven.
- Why do men pass gas more than woman? Because women can't shut up long enough to build up the required pressure.
- If your dog is barking at the back door and your wife is yelling at the front door, who do you let in first? The dog, of course, will shut up once you let it in.
- What's worse than a Male Chauvinist Pig? A woman who won't do what she's told.
- I married Miss Right. I just didn't know her first name was *Always*.
- Scientists have discovered a food that diminishes a woman's sex drive by 90%: a wedding cake.
- Why do men die before their wives? They want to.
- In the beginning, God created the earth and rested. Then God created man and rested. Then God created woman . . . **Since then, neither God nor Man has rested.**

13

ANSWERS TO QUESTIONNAIRE (designed to learn more about your friends) 'BEST' email from John of NYC.

Question ★ ★ ★ Answer

	Question	Answer
1.	What time is it?	Too late for me
2.	Name?	Mudd
3.	What are you most afraid of?	Breathing
4.	What do you drive?	People crazy
5.	Have you ever seen a ghost?	Every morning in the mirror
6.	Where were you born?	On a warm summer's eve
7.	Ever been to Alaska?	Must reference map; was glacier in previous life
8.	Ever been toilet papering?	What's toilet paper?
9.	Croutons or bacon bits?	Bruins
10.	Favorite day of the week?	Heyday
11.	Favorite restaurant?	American Airlines - Coach
12.	Favorite flower?	Billie Jo
13.	Favorite sport to watch?	George Bush spikkin Engrich
14.	Favorite drink?	Thine eyes
15.	Favorite ice cream?	Over easy
16.	Favorite fast food restaurant?	Cucina Las Cucarachas Grande
17.	What color is your bedroom carpet?	Unable to discern through blood stains
18.	Times you have failed your driver's test?	Once, but I was drunk
19.	From whom did you get your last email?	Penis reduction pills
20.	What do you do when you are bored?	Look for the prize at the bottom of whiskey bottles
21.	Bedtime?	Uncertain - am currently asleep
22.	Who will respond to this email the quickest?	Do you mean most quickly?
23.	Who is the person you sent this to that is least likely to respond?	My third personality
24.	Who is the person that you are most curious to see their responses?	My fourth personality

25. Favorite TV show?   Mix-O-Matic Dicer
                                                       available 4 payments of
                                                       $29.99; that's 4
                                                       payments of $29.99
26. Ford or Chevy?   Schwinn
27. What are your favorite colors?   Black and Decker
28. How many tattoos do you have?   437.03 (sorry, I wasn't
                                                       thinking)
29. Do you have any pets?   One pet peeve
30. Which came first the chicken or the egg? Please, no more sex talk
31. What would you like to accomplish before
    you die?   Immortality
32. To how many people are you sending   Billie Jo is a person?!
    this email?

THOUGHT FOR THE DAY - MONKEYS

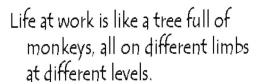

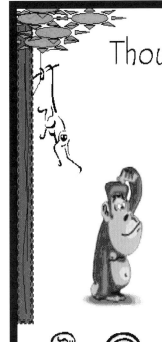

Thought for the day…

Life at work is like a tree full of monkeys, all on different limbs at different levels.

Some monkeys are climbing up, some down.

The monkeys on top look down and see a tree full of smiling faces.

The monkeys on the bottom look up and see nothing but assholes.

15

WHAT DOES LOVE MEAN?

A group of professionals posed this question to a group of 4 to 8 year olds "What does love mean?"

When my grandmother got arthritis, she couldn't bend over to paint her toenails so my grandfather does it for her all the time, even when his hands got arthritis too. That's love. (Becca-age 8)

When someone loves you, the way they say your name is different. You just know that your name is safe in their mouth. (Billy-age 4)

Love is when a girl puts on perfume and a boy puts on shaving cologne and they go out and smell each other. (Karl-age 5)

Love is when you go out to eat and give somebody most of your French fries without making them give you any of theirs. (Chrissy-age 6)

Love is when my mommy makes coffee for my daddy and she takes a sip to make sure that it tastes OK. (Danny-age 7)

Love is what's in the room with you at Christmas, if you stop opening presents and listen. (Bobby-age 7)

If you want to learn to love better, you should start with a friend who you hate. (Nikka-age 6)

Love is like a little old woman and a little old man who are still friends even after they know each other so well. (Tommy-age 6)

My mommy loves me more than anybody. You don't see anyone else kissing me to sleep at night. (Claire-age 6)

Love is when mommy sees daddy all smelly and sweaty and still says he is more handsome than Robert Redford. (Chris-age 7)

Love is when your puppy licks your face even after you left him alone all day. (MaryAnn-age 4)

I know my older sister loves me because she gives me all her old clothes and has to go out and buy new ones! (Lauren-age 4)

When you love somebody your eyelashes go up and down; little stars come out of you. (Karen-age 7)

 Our winner was a 4 year old boy: A 4 year old child's next door neighbor was an elderly gentleman who had recently lost his wife. Upon seeing the man cry, the little boy went into the old gentleman's yard, climbed onto his lap and just sat there. When his Mother asked what he had said to the neighbor the little boy said, "Nothing, I just helped him cry."

16

STRESS DIET TO HELP WOMAN COPE

This is a specially formulated diet designed to help women cope with the stress that builds during the day.

Breakfast: 1 grapefruit, 1 slice whole wheat toast, 1 cup skim milk

Lunch: 1 sm portion poached chicken, 1 cup spinach, 1 cup herbal tea, 1 Hershey's Kiss

Afternoon: The rest of the Hershey Kisses in the bag, 1 tub of Hagen-Daaz Ice Cream

Dinner: 4 glasses of wine, 2 loaves of garlic bread, 1 large pizza, 3 Snickers Bars

Late Night: 1 whole Sara Lee cheesecake

S T R E S S E D spelled backwards is D E S S E R T S

BLONDE – DRIVER'S LICENSE

A police officer stops a blonde for speeding and asks her, very nicely, if he could see her license. She replied in a huff, "I wish you guys would get your act together. Just yesterday you took my license away and then today you expect me to show it to you?"

SIGNS - SIGNS OF WHAT?

AMAZING - READ THIS

Fi yuo can raed this, yuo hvae a sgtrane mnid too. Cna yuo raed tihs? Olny 55 plepoe can. I cdnuolt blveiee taht I cluod aulaclty uesdnatnrd waht I was rdanieg. The phaonmneal pweor of the human mnid, aoccdrnig to a rscheearch at Cmabrigde Uinervtisy, it dseno't mtaetr in waht oerdr the ltteres in a wrod are, the olny ipromtnt tihng is taht the frsit and lsat ltteer be in the rghit pclae. The rset can be a taotl mses and you can sitll raed it whotuit a pboerlm. Tihs is bcuseae the huamn mnid deos not raed ervey lteter by istlef, but the wrod as a wlohe. Azanmig huh? Yaeh, and I awlyas tghuhot slpeling was ipmorantt!

18

CALIFORNIANS

So as not to be outdone by all the redneck, hillbilly and Texan jokes, you know you're from California if:

- Your co-worker has 8 body piercings and none of them are visible.
- You make over $400,000 and still can't afford a house.
- You take a bus and are shocked at two people carrying on a conversation in English.
- Your child's 3rd grade teacher has purple hair, a nose ring and is named Flower.
- You can't remember… is pot illegal?
- You've been to a baby shower that has two mothers and a sperm donor.
- You have a very strong opinion about where your coffee beans are grown and you can taste the difference between Sumatran and Ethiopian.
- You can't remember… is pot illegal?
- A really great parking space can totally move you to tears.
- Gas costs $1.00 per gallon more than anywhere else in the United States.
- Unlike back home, the guy at 8:30 am at Starbucks wearing a baseball cap and sunglasses who looks like George Clooney really *IS* George Clooney.
- Your car insurance costs as much as your house payment.
- You can't remember… is pot illegal?
- It's barely sprinkling rain and there's a report on every news station: 'STORM WATCH'.
- You pass an elementary school playground and the children are all busy with their cell phones or pagers.
- It's barely sprinkling rain outside, so you leave for work an hour early to avoid all the 'weather-related' accidents.
- HEY!!! Is pot illegal???
- Both you AND your dog have therapists.
- The Terminator is your Governor.
- If you drive illegally, they take your driver's license away. If you're here illegally, they want to give you one.

Sissy crap

None of that Sissy Crap! Are you tired of those sissy 'friendship' poems that always sound good, but never actually come close to reality? Well, here is a series of promises that actually speak of true friendship. The stone cold truth of great friendship:

- When you are sad, I will help you get drunk and plot revenge against the sorry bastard who made you sad.
- When you are blue, I will try to dislodge whatever is choking you.
- When you smile, I will know you finally got laid.
- When you are scared, I will rag on you about it every chance I get.
- When you are worried, I will tell you horrible stories about how much worse it could be until you quit whining.
- When you are confused, I will use little words.
- When you are sick, stay the hell away from me until you are well again. I don't want whatever you have.
- When you fall, I will point and laugh at your clumsy ass.

Friendship is like peeing your pants, everyone can see it, but only you can feel the true warmth. And always remember... when life hands you lemons, ask for tequila and salt and call me over!!!

Photos - that's cool!

Porn for women - a gift from man

"I know, lets take you shoe shopping!"
"Is that the baby crying? I'll get her."
"I like to get to the chores before I have to be asked."
"As long as I have legs, you'll never have to take the garbage out."
"I don't have to have a reason to bring you flowers."
"Ooh the NFL playoffs are today. I bet we'll have no trouble parking at the crafts fair."
"I made some lamb tenderloin for dinner. I hope that sounds okay."
"Hold that thought a second. I want to pull over to ask for directions."

20

PHOTOS - MOTHER OF THE YEAR

In a California zoo a mother tiger gave birth to a rare set of triplet tiger cubs. Unfortunately, due to complications, the cubs died shortly after birth. The mother tiger suddenly started to decline in health although she was physically fine. The zoo felt the loss of her litter caused her to fall into depression. The doctors decided she might improve if she could surrogate another mother's cubs.

After checking with many other zoos, the disappointing news was that there were no tiger cubs of the right age to introduce to the mourning mother. The veterinarians decided to try something that had never been tried in a zoo environment. The only orphans that could be found quickly were a litter of piglets. The zoo keepers and vets wrapped the piglets in tiger skin and placed the babies around the mother tiger.

Would they become cubs or pork chops??

REFLECTIONS - MY NAME IS ROSE

The first day of school our professor introduced himself and challenged us to get to know someone we didn't already know. I stood up to look around when a gentle hand touched my shoulder. I turned around to find a wrinkled, little old lady beaming up at me with a smile that lit up her entire being. She said, "Hi handsome. My name is **ROSE**. I'm eighty-seven years old. Can I give you a hug?" I laughed and enthusiastically responded, "Of course you may!" and she gave me a giant squeeze.

"Why are you in college at such a young, innocent age?" I asked. She jokingly replied, "I'm here to meet a rich husband, get married and have a couple of kids." "No seriously," I asked. I was curious what may have motivated her to be taking on this challenge at her age. "I always dreamed of having a college education and now I'm getting one!" she told me.

After class we walked to the student union building and shared a chocolate milk shake. We became instant friends. Everyday for the next three months we would leave class together and talk nonstop. I was always mesmerized listening to this 'time machine' as she shared her wisdom and experience with me. Over the course of the year, Rose became a campus icon and she easily made friends wherever she went. She loved to dress up and she reveled in the attention bestowed upon her from the other students. She was living it up.

At the end of the semester we invited Rose to speak at our football banquet. I'll never forget what she taught us. She was introduced and stepped up to the podium. As she began to deliver her prepared speech she dropped her three by five cards on the floor. Frustrated and a little embarrassed she leaned into the microphone and simply said, "I'm sorry I'm so jittery. I gave up beer for Lent and this whiskey is killing me! I'll never get my speech back in order so let me just tell you what I know." As we laughed she cleared her throat and began: *"We do not stop playing because we are old; we grow old because we stop playing.*

There are only four secrets to staying young, being happy and achieving success. You have to laugh and find humor every day. You've got to have a dream. When you lose your dreams, you die. We have so many people walking around who are dead and don't even know it!

There is a huge difference between growing older and growing up. If you are nineteen years old and lie in bed for one full year and don't do one productive thing, you will turn twenty years old. If I am eighty-seven years old and stay in bed for a year and never do anything, I will turn eighty-eight.

Anyone can grow older. That doesn't take any talent or ability. The idea is to grow up by always finding opportunity in change. Have no regrets. The elderly usually don't have regrets for what we did, but rather for things we did not do. The only people who fear death are those with regrets."

She concluded her speech by courageously singing 'The Rose'.
She challenged each of us to study the lyrics and live them out in our daily lives. At the year's end Rose finished the college degree she had begun all those years ago. One week after graduation Rose died peacefully in her sleep. Over two thousand college students attended her funeral in tribute to the wonderful woman who taught by example that it's never too late to be all you can possibly be. These words have been passed along in loving memory of **ROSE**.

REMEMBER, GROWING OLDER IS MANDATORY. GROWING UP IS OPTIONAL.

PHOTOS - AIRPORT CAMEL

22 GENERAL 'TRUTHS'

1. Do not walk behind me for I may not lead. Do not walk ahead of me for I may not follow. Do not walk beside me either. Just pretty much leave me alone.
2. The journey of a thousand miles begins with a broken fan belt and leaky tires.
3. It is always darkest before dawn. So if you are going to steal your neighbor's newspaper, that's the time to do it.
4. Don't be irreplaceable. If you can't be replaced, you can't be promoted.
5. Always remember that you are unique. Just like everyone else.
6. Never test the depth of the water with both feet.
7. If you think nobody cares if you are alive, try missing a couple of car payments.
8. Before you criticize someone, you should walk a mile in their shoes. That way when you criticize them, you are a mile away and you have their shoes.
9. If at first you don't succeed, sky diving is not for you.
10. Give a man a fish and he will eat for a day. Teach him how to fish and he will sit in a boat and drink beer all day.
11. If you lend someone $20 and never see that person again, it is probably worth it.
12. If you tell the truth, you don't have to remember anything.
13. Some days you are the bug; some days you are the windshield.
14. Everyone seems normal until you get to know them.
15. The quickest way to double your money is to fold it and put it back in your pocket.
16. A closed mouth gathers no foot.
17. Duct tape is like 'the force'. It has a light side, a dark side and it holds the universe together.
18. There are two theories to arguing with women. Neither one works.
19. Generally speaking, you aren't learning much when your lips are moving.
20. Experience is something you don't get until just after you need it.
21. Never miss a good chance to shut up.
22. Never ever take a sleeping pill and a laxative on the same night.

THE NEW RED HAT

An older lady was standing at the railing of the cruise ship holding her hat tight so it would not blow away in the wind. A gentleman approached her and said, "Pardon me, madam. I do not intend to be forward but did you know your dress is blowing up in the high wind?" "Yes, I know," said the lady. "I need both hands to hold onto this hat." "But madam, you must know that you are not wearing any panties and your privates are exposed!" said the gentleman in earnest. The woman looked down, then back up at the man and replied, "Sir, anything you see down there is 85 years old. I just bought this hat yesterday!"

Though no one can go back and make a brand new start, anyone can start from now and make a brand new ending. One of the hardest things in life to learn is which bridge to cross and which bridge to burn.

ONLY IN TEXAS

A cowboy from Houston gets pulled over by a Texas State Trooper for speeding. The trooper started to lecture the cowboy about his speeding and in general began to throw his weight around to try to make the cowboy feel uncomfortable. Finally the trooper got around to writing the ticket. As he was doing that, he kept swatting at some flies that were buzzing around his head.

The cowboy says, "Y'all havin' some problems with them circle flies?" The trooper stopped writing the ticket and said, "Well yeah, if that's what they're called. But I've never heard of circle flies." "Well, sir," the cowboy replies, "circle flies hang around ranches. They're called circle flies because they are almost always found circling around the back end of a horse."

The trooper says, "Oh," and goes back to writing the ticket. But a moment later he stops and asks, "Are you callin' me a horse's ass?" "No, sir," the cowboy replies, "I have too much respect for law enforcement to call y'all a horse's ass." "That's a good thing," the trooper says and goes back to writing the ticket. After a long pause, the cowboy, in his best Texas drawl says, *"Hard to fool them flies though."*

PHOTOS - A CHINESE TOY RECALL

WOMEN'S REVENGE

"Cash, check or charge?" the sales girl asked, after folding items Bella wished to purchase. As Bella fumbled for her wallet the clerk noticed a remote control for a TV set in Bella's purse. "So do you always carry your TV remote?" the clerk asked. "No," Bella replied, "but my boyfriend refused to come shopping with me and I figured this was the most evil thing I could do to him, legally."

PHOTOS - BOOBIES (think these Chicks are related)?

Women at Mardi Gras   **Banned from Disneyland**

MARRIAGE SEMINAR

While attending a marriage seminar, dealing with communication, Uncle Howard and his wife, Aunt Juanda, listened to the instructor. "It is essential that husbands and wives know each other's likes and dislikes." The instructor asked Uncle Howard, "Can you name your wife's favorite flower?" Uncle Howard leaned over, touched Aunt Juanda's arm gently and whispered, **"It's Pillsbury, isn't it?"**

WORDS

A husband read an article to his wife about how many words women use a day... 30,000 compared to a man's 15,000. The wife replied, "The reason has to be because we have to repeat everything to men." The husband then turned to his wife and asked, "What?"

PRISON vs WORK

IN PRISON	AT WORK
You spend the majority of your time in a 10x10 cell.	You spend the majority of your time in an 8 x 8 cubicle.
You get three meals a day fully paid for.	You get a break for one meal and you have to pay for it.
You get time off for good behavior.	You get more work for good behavior.
The guard locks and unlocks all the doors for you.	You must often carry a security card and open all the doors for yourself.
You can watch TV and play games.	You could get fired for watching TV and playing games.
You get your own toilet.	You have to share the toilet with someone who pees on the seat.
They allow your family and friends to visit.	You aren't even supposed to speak to your family.
All expenses are paid by the taxpayers with no work required.	You get to pay all your expenses to go to work and they deduct taxes from your salary to pay for prisoners and welfare.
You spend most of your life inside bars wanting to get out.	You spend most of your time wanting to get out and go inside bars.
You must deal with sadistic wardens.	At work they are called managers.

CARTOONS - MAMMOGRAMS . . .

I HAD MY PHYSICAL TODAY

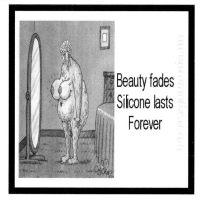

RELATIVES

A couple drove down a country road for several miles not saying a word. An earlier discussion had led to an argument and neither of them wanted to concede their position. As they passed a barnyard of mules, goats and pigs the husband asked sarcastically, "Relatives of yours?" "Yep," the wife responded, **"In-laws."**

SIGNS - THE COUNTRY STORE

THE SILENT TREATMENT

Moe and Parvaneh were having some problems at home and were giving each other the silent treatment. Suddenly Moe realized that the next day he would need Parvaneh to wake him at 5:00 am for an early morning business flight. Not wanting to be the first to break the silence (and LOSE), Moe wrote on a piece of paper, "Please wake me at 5:00am." He left it where he knew she would find it. The next morning the Moe woke up only to discover it was 9:00 am. Moe had missed his flight and was furious. He was about to go and see why Parvaneh hadn't wakened him, when he noticed a piece of paper by the bed. The paper read, "It's 5:00am. Wake up." **Men are not equipped for this kind of contest.**

PHOTOS - NEIGHBORS TOPIARY

GIVING UP WINE

Billie was walking down the street when she was accosted by a particularly dirty and shabby looking homeless woman who asked her for a couple of dollars for dinner. She took out her wallet, got out ten dollars and asked, "If I give you this money will you buy some wine with it instead of dinner?" "No, I had to stop drinking years ago," the homeless woman told Billie. "Will you use it to go shopping instead of buying food?" she asked. "No, I don't waste time shopping," the homeless woman said. "I need to spend all my time trying to stay alive." "Will you spend this on a beauty salon instead of food?" she asked. "Are you nuts?" replied the homeless woman. "I haven't had my hair done in 20 years!" "Well," Billie said, "I'm not going to give you the money. Instead I'm going to take you out for dinner with my husband and me tonight." The homeless woman was shocked. "Won't your husband be furious with you for doing that? I know I'm dirty and I probably smell pretty disgusting." Billie said, "That's okay. *It's important for him to see what a woman looks like after she has given up shopping, hair appointments and wine!*"

(Gwen, what are these 'blank' pages costing? bjm)

CHAPTER 2

FIRST DATE (Jay Leno)

This is probably the funniest 'first date' story ever. It was first seen on the *Tonight Show*. Jay Leno went into the audience to find the most embarrassing first date that a woman ever had.

She said it was midwinter, snowing and quite cold. The guy had taken her skiing in the mountains outside Salt Lake City, UT. It was a day trip (no overnight). They were strangers and truly had never met before. The outing was fun but relatively uneventful until they were headed home late that afternoon. They were driving back down the mountain when she gradually began to realize that she should not have had that extra latte. They were about an hour away from anywhere with a rest room and in the middle of nowhere. Her companion suggested she try to hold it, which she did for a while. Unfortunately, because of the heavy snow and slow going, there came a point where she told him he had better stop and let her go beside the road or it would be the front seat of his car. They stopped and she quickly crawled out beside the car, yanked her pants down and started. In the deep snow she didn't have good footing so she let her butt rest against the rear fender to steady herself. Her companion stood at the side of the car watching for traffic and indeed was a real gentleman and refrained from peeking. All she could think about was the relief she felt despite the rather embarrassing nature of the situation.

Upon finishing, however, she soon became aware of another sensation. As she bent to pull up her pants, the young lady discovered her buttocks were firmly glued against the car's fender. Thoughts of tongues frozen to poles immediately came to mind as she attempted to disengage her flesh from the icy metal. It was quickly apparent that she had a brand new problem due to the extreme cold. Horrified by her plight, and yet aware of the humor of the moment, she answered her date's concerns about 'what's taking so long' with a reply that indeed she was 'freezing her butt off' and in need of some assistance!!! He came around the car as she tried to cover herself with her sweater and then, as she looked imploringly into

34

his eyes, he burst out laughing. She too got the giggles and when they finally composed themselves, they assessed her dilemma. Obviously, as hysterical as the situation was, they also were faced with a real problem. Both agreed it would take something hot to free her chilly cheeks from the grip of the icy metal! Thinking about what had gotten her into the predicament in the first place, both quickly realized that there was only one way to get her free. So as she looked the other way, her first-time date proceeded to unzip his pants and pee her butt off the fender.

As the audience screamed in laughter, she took the *Tonight Show's* prize hands down .... or perhaps that should be pants down! And you thought your first date was embarrassing. Jay Leno's comment 'this gives a whole new meaning to being pissed off'.

PHOTOS - BABIES (can't get enough)

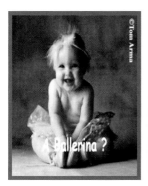

REFLECTIONS - OLD AGE IS A GIFT

The other day a young person asked me how I felt about being old. I was surprised for I do not think of myself as old. Upon seeing my reaction, she was immediately embarrassed. I explained it was an interesting question and that I would ponder it and let her know. *Old age, I decided is a gift.* I am now, probably for the first time in my life, the person I have always wanted to be. Oh, not my body! I sometimes despair over my body: the wrinkles, the baggy eyes and the sagging butt. Often I am taken aback by that old person that lives in my mirror, who looks like my mother! I don't agonize over those things for long.

I would never trade my amazing friends, my wonderful life or my loving family for less gray hair or a flatter belly. As I've aged, I've become more kind to myself and less critical of myself. I've become my own friend. I don't chide myself for eating that extra cookie, for not making my bed, for buying that silly cement gecko that I didn't need but that looks so adorable on my patio. I am entitled to a treat, to be messy, to be extravagant. I have seen too many dear friends leave this world too soon; before they understood the great freedom that comes with aging.

Whose business is it if I choose to read or play on the computer until 4am and sleep until noon? I will dance with myself to those wonderful tunes of the 60's and 70's and if I, at the same time, wish to weep over a lost love I will. I will walk the beach in a swim suit that is stretched over a bulging body and will dive into the waves with abandon if I choose to, despite the pitying glances from the jet set. They, too, will get old.

I know I am sometimes forgetful. But then again, some of life is just as well forgotten. I eventually remember the important things. Sure, over the years my heart has been broken. How can your heart not break when you lose a loved one or when a child suffers or even when somebody's beloved pet gets hit by a car? Broken hearts are what give us strength, understanding and compassion. A heart never broken is pristine and sterile and will never know the joy of being imperfect. I am blessed to have lived long enough to have my hair turn gray and my youthful laughs be forever etched into deep grooves on my face. So many have never laughed and so many have died before their hair could turn silver. As you get older it is easier to be positive. You care less about what other people think, you don't question yourself anymore and you have earned the right to be wrong.

So, to answer the question, I like being old, as it has set me free. I like the person I have become. I am not going to live forever but while I am still here I will not waste time lamenting what could have been or worry about what will be. I shall eat dessert every single day (if I feel like it). *May our friendship never come apart especially when it is straight from the heart! May you always have a rainbow of smiles on your face and in your heart.* **FRIENDS FOREVER.**

PHOTOS - MONA LISA (AFTER ONE WEEK IN L.A.)!

THOUGHT FOR THE DAY - PIG

A very short story: Man driving down the road. Woman driving up same road. They pass each other. The woman yells out the window, "PIG!" The man yells out the window, "BITCH!" Man rounds next curve and crashes into a HUGE PIG in the middle of the road and dies. **If only men would listen.**

TEN WAYS TO TELL IF YOUR MAN HAS 'DONE TIME'

1. Keeps all his worldly possessions in a cardboard box beside the bed.
2. Insists on making a clothes line or privacy screen around the bed from ripped up sheets.
3. Woofs down his dinner in 3 minutes and knocks on the table top when he's done.
4. Wears his headphones when he watches TV.
5. Constantly talks about his 'homies & crimeys'.
6. Refers to your local grocery store as 'the canteen'.
7. Uses Irish Spring for shampoo.
8. Showers wearing his boxers and flip flops.
9. Washes his socks in the shower.
10. Is covered with tattoos that look like they were drawn by a 4 year old wearing socks on his hands.

OSAMA BIN LADEN in PAKISTAN

While trying to escape through Pakistan, Osama Bin Laden found a bottle on the sand and picked it up. Suddenly a female Genie rose from the bottle and with a smile said, "Master, may I grant you one wish?" Osama responded, "You ignorant, unworthy daughter-of-a-dog, don't you know who I am? I don't need any common woman giving me anything." The shocked Genie said, "Please, I must grant you a wish or I will be returned to that bottle forever." Osama thought a moment, then grumbled about the impertinence of the woman and said, "Very well, I want to awaken with three American women in my bed in the morning. So just do it and be off with yourself." The annoyed Genie said, "So be it," and disappeared. The next morning Osama Bin Laden woke up in bed with Lorena Bobbitt, Tonya Harding and Hillary Clinton at his side. His penis was gone, his knees were broken and he had no health insurance. **God is Good.**

Signs - SIGNS OF WHAT?

Reflections - BEGIN LIFE RIGHT NOW

As we grow up we learn that even the one person that wasn't supposed to ever let you down probably will. You will have your heart broken more than once and it's harder every time. You'll break hearts, too, so remember how it felt when yours was broken. You'll fight with your best friend. You'll blame a new love for things an old one did. You'll cry because time is passing too fast and you'll eventually lose someone you love. So take too many pictures, laugh too much and love like you've never been hurt because every sixty seconds you spend upset, is a minute of happiness you'll never get back. Don't be afraid that your life will end, be afraid that it will never begin.

waiting for your ship to come in

39

QUESTIONS TO THINK ABOUT

- Can you cry under water?
- How important does a person have to be before they are considered assassinated instead of just murdered?
- Why do you have to 'put your two cents in' . . . but it's only a 'penny for your thoughts'? Where's that extra penny going?
- Once you're in heaven, do you get stuck wearing the clothes you were buried in for eternity?
- Why does a round pizza come in a square box?
- What disease did cured ham actually have?
- How is it that we put man on the moon before we figured out how to put wheels on luggage?
- Why is it that people say they 'slept like a baby' when babies wake up like every two hours?
- If a deaf person has to go to court, is it still called a hearing?
- Why are you IN a movie, but you are ON TV?
- Why do doctors leave the room while you get dressed... they will see you naked anyway.
- Why is 'bra' singular and 'panties' plural?
- Why do toasters always have a setting that burns the toast to a horrible crisp, which no one would ever eat?
- Can a hearse, carrying a corpse, drive in the carpool lane?
- If the professor on Gilligan's Island could make a radio out of a coconut, why couldn't he fix a hole in a boat?
- Why does Goofy stand erect while Pluto remains on all fours? They're both dogs...
- If corn oil is made from corn, vegetable oil is made from vegetables, what is baby oil made from?
- Does the Alphabet song and Twinkle, Twinkle Little Star have the same tune?
- Did you ever notice that when you blow in your dog's face he gets mad at you, but when you take him for a car ride he sticks his head out the window?
- *Do you ever wonder why you gave me you're e-mail address in the first place?*

40

MAN NEVER UNDERSTANDS WOMAN

I know I'm not ever going to understand a woman. I'll never understand how you can take boiling hot wax, smear it on your bikini line, rip the hair out by the root and still be afraid of a spider.

PSYCHIATRIST'S ANALYSIS (WHAT'S IN A NAME?)

A psychiatrist was conducting a group therapy session with four young mothers and their small children. "You all have obsessions," he observed. To the first mother, Amy, he said "You are obsessed with eating. You've even named your daughter Candy." He turned to the second Mom, Diana, "Your obsession is with money. Again, it manifests itself in your child's name, Penny." He turned to the third Mom, Sara, "Your obsession is alcohol. This too shows itself in your child's name, Brandy". At this point the fourth mother, Kerry, quietly got up, took her little boy by the hand and whispered, "Come on Dick, we're leaving."

PHOTOS - FATHER'S DAY

41

PHOTOS - SIBLING RIVALRY: HOW TO TELL IF YOU ARE MOM'S FAVORITE

THREE ITALIAN NUNS

At the Pearly Gates, they are met by St. Peter who says, "Sisters, you all led such exemplary lives the Lord is granting you six months to go back to earth and be anyone you wish to be."

The first nun says, "I want to be Sophia Loren" and 'poof' she's gone. The second nun says, "I want to be Madonna" and 'poof' she's gone. The third nun says, "I want to be Sara Pipaline..."

St. Peter looks perplexed and asks, "Who?" "Sara Pipaline," replies the nun. St. Peter shakes his head and says, "I'm sorry but that name just doesn't ring a bell." The nun takes a newspaper out of her habit and hands it to St. Peter. St. Peter reads the paper and chuckles. He hands it back to her and says, "No sister, the paper says it was the 'Sahara Pipeline' that was 'laid by 1,400 men in 6 months'."

42

CARTOONS - CUTE SEXY

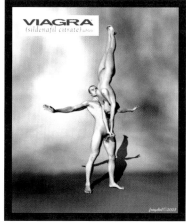

43

POEM FROM SON TO MOM and FROM MOM TO SON

Son's Poem

My son came home from school one day, with a smirk upon his face
He decided he was smart enough, to put me in my place

Guess what I learned in Civics Two that's taught by Mr. Wright
It's all about the laws today, the Children's Bill of Rights

It says, I need not clean my room, don't have to cut my hair
No one can tell me what to think, or speak, or what to wear

I have freedom from religion and regardless of what you say
I don't have to bow my head and I sure don't have to pray

I can wear earrings if I want and pierce my tongue and nose
I can read and watch just what I like, get tattoos from head to toe

And if you ever spank me, I'll charge you with a crime
I'll back up all my charges with the marks on my behind

Don't you ever touch me, my body's only for my use
Not for your hugs and kisses, that's just more child abuse

Don't preach about your morals like your Mama did to you
That's nothing more than mind control and that's illegal too

Mom, I have these children's right so you can't influence me
Or I'll call Children's Services Division, better known as C.S.D.

Mom's Reply

Of course my first instinct was to toss him out the door
But the chance to teach him a lesson made me think a little more

I mulled it over carefully, I couldn't let this go
A smile crept upon my face; he's messing with a pro

Next day I took him shopping at the local Goodwill Store
I told him, pick out all you want, there are shirts and pants galore

I've called and checked with C.S.D., who said they didn't care
If I bought you K-Mart shoes instead of those Nike Airs

I've cancelled that appointment to take your driver's test
The C.S.D. is unconcerned, so I'll decide what's best

I said, no time to stop and eat or pick up stuff to munch
And tomorrow you can start to learn to make you own sack lunch

Just save the raging appetite and wait 'til dinner time
We're having liver and onions, a favorite dish of mine

He asked, can I please rent a movie to watch on my VCR?
Sorry, but I sold your TV for new tires on my car
I also rented out your room; you'll take the couch instead
The C.S.D. requires just a roof over your head

Your clothing won't be trendy now; I'll choose what we eat
That allowance that you used to get will buy me something neat

I'm selling off your jet ski, dirt bide and roller blades
Check out the Parents Bill of Rights, it's in effect today

Hey hot shot, are you crying? Why are you on your knees?
Are you asking God to help you out, please?

45

PHOTOS - ADORABLE DOGS

3 YEAR OLD GIRL'S PRAYER

A father put his 3 year old daughter to bed, told her a short story and listened to her prayers which ended, "God bless Mommy, God bless Daddy, God bless Grandma and good-bye Grandpa." The father asked, "Why did you say good-bye Grandpa?" The little girl said, "I don't know Daddy, it just seemed like the thing to do." The next day grandpa died. The father thought it was a strange coincidence.

A few months later the father put his daughter to bed and listened to her prayers which finished with, "And God Bless Mommy, God Bless Daddy and good-bye Grandma." The next day the child's grandmother died. "Oh my gosh," thought the father, " this kid is in contact with the other side."

Several weeks later when the girl was going to bed the dad heard her say, "God bless Mommy and good-bye Daddy." He practically went into shock. He couldn't sleep all night. He got up at the crack of dawn to go to his office. He was nervous as a cat all day, had lunch and watched the clock. He figured if he could get by until midnight he would be okay. He felt safe in the office so instead of going home at the end of the day he stayed there, drinking coffee, looking at his watch and jumping at every sound. Finally, midnight arrived, he breathed a sigh of relief and went home.

When he got home his wife said, "I've never seen you work so late, what's the matter?" He said, "I don't want to talk about it, I've just spent the worst day of my life." She said, "You think you had a bad day, you'll never believe what happened to me. **This morning my golf pro dropped dead in the middle of my lesson!"**

46

REFLECTIONS - I LOVE YOU

One day a woman's husband died and on that clear, cold morning, in the warmth of their bedroom, the wife was struck with the pain of learning that sometimes there isn't anymore: no more hugs, no more special moments to celebrate together, no more phone calls just to chat, no more 'just one minute'. Sometimes, what we care about the most gets all used up and goes away, never to return before we can say good-bye or 'I love you'. So while we have it, it is best we love it, care for it, heal it when it's sick and fix it when it's broken. This is true for marriage, old cars, and children with bad report cards, dogs with bad hips, aging parents and grandparents. We keep them because they are worth it, because we are worth it. Some things we keep, like a best friend who moved away or a classmate we grew up with. There are just some things that make us happy no matter what. Life is important, like people we know who are special, and so we keep them close. Suppose one morning you did not wake up. Do all your friends know you love them? I was thinking, I could die today, tomorrow or next week and wondered if I had any wounds needing to be healed, friendships that needed re-kindling or three words needing to be said: **I LOVE YOU. . .**

BLONDE - DEODORANT

Katherine, a blonde, walks into a pharmacy and asks for some rectum deodorant. George, the pharmacist, a little bemused, explained to the woman that they don't sell rectum deodorant and never have. Unfazed, Katherine assures George that she has been buying the stuff from this store on a regular basis and would like some more. "I'm sorry," says the pharmacist, "we don't have any." "But I always buy it here," says the blonde. "Do you have the container it came in?" asks George. "Yes," said Katherine, "I'll go home and get it." She returns with the container and hands it to the pharmacist who looks at it and says to her, "This is just a normal stick of underarm deodorant." Annoyed, Katherine snatches the container back and reads out loud from the container . . ."*TO APPLY, PUSH UP BOTTOM.*"

DIVORCE LETTER

Dear Wife:

I'm writing you this letter to tell you I'm leaving you for good. I've been a good man to you for seven years and I have nothing to show for it. These last two weeks have been hell.

Your boss called to tell me that you had quit your job today and that was the last straw. Last week you came home and didn't even notice that I had gotten a new hair cut, cooked your favorite meal and even wore a brand new pair of silk boxers. You came home, ate in two minutes and went straight to sleep after watching all of your soaps. You don't tell me you love me anymore, you don't want sex anymore. Either you're cheating on me or you don't love me anymore. Whatever the case, I'm GONE!

Signed: Your Ex-Husband

P.S. Don't try to find me. Your sister and I are moving to West Virginia together. Have a great life.

Dear Ex-Husband:

Nothing has made my day more than receiving your letter. It's true that you and I have been married for seven years, although a good man is a far cry from what you've been.

I watch my soaps so much because they drown out your constant whining and griping. Too bad that doesn't work. I did notice when you got a hair cut last week, the first thing that came to mind was 'you look just like a girl' but my mother raised me not to say anything if you can't say something nice. And when you cooked my favorite meal, you must have gotten me confused with my sister. I stopped eating pork seven years ago. I turned away from you when you had those new silk boxers on because the price tag was still on them. I prayed that it was a coincidence that my sister had just borrowed fifty dollars from me that morning (your silk boxers were $49.99).

After all of this, I still loved you and felt that we could work it out. So when I discovered that I had hit the lotto for ten million dollars, I quit my job and bought us two tickets to Jamaica. BUT when I got home you were gone. Everything happens for a reason I guess. I hope you have the fulfilling life you've always wanted. My lawyer said with the letter you wrote, you won't get a dime from me. So take care.

Signed: RICH and FREE

P.S. I don't know if I ever told you this but Carla, my sister, was born Carl. I hope that's not a problem.

BLONDE - VACUUM

A blonde was playing Trivial Pursuit one night. It was her turn. She rolled the dice and she landed on Science & Nature. Her question was, "If you are in a vacuum and someone calls your name, can you hear it?" She thought for a moment and then asked, "Is the vacuum off or on?"

REFLECTIONS - REALIZE THE VALUE OF TIME

To realize the value of a sister, ask someone who doesn't have one
To realize the value of ten years, ask a newly divorced couple
To realize the value of one year, ask a student who has failed a final exam
To realize the value of nine months, ask a mother who gave birth to a stillborn baby
To realize the value of one month, ask a mother who has a premature baby
To realize the value of one week, ask an editor of a weekly newspaper
To realize the value of one minute, ask a person who has missed the train, bus or a plane
To realize the value of one second, ask a person who has survived an accident
To realize the value of a friend or family member, lose one

Time waits for no one; treasure every moment you have

23 UNANSWERED QUESTIONS

1. Ever wonder about those people who spend $2.00 a piece on those little bottles of Evian water? Evian spelled backwards = NAIVE

2. Isn't making a smoking section in a restaurant like making a peeing section in a swimming pool?

3. If 4 out of 5 people SUFFER from diarrhea... does that mean that one person enjoys it?

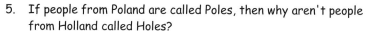

4. There are three religious truths: (a) Jews do not recognize Jesus as the Messiah; (b) Protestants do not recognize the Pope as the leader of the Christian faith; and (c) Baptists do not recognize each other in the liquor store or at Hooters.

5. If people from Poland are called Poles, then why aren't people from Holland called Holes?

6. Do infants enjoy infancy as much as adults enjoy adultery?

7. If a pig loses its voice, is it disgruntled?

8. Why do croutons come in airtight packages... aren't they just stale bread to begin with?

9. Why is a person who plays the piano called a pianist but a person who drives a racecar is not called a racist?

10. Why isn't the number 11 pronounced onety-one?

11. If lawyers are disbarred and clergymen defrocked, then doesn't it follow that electricians can be delighted, musicians denoted, cowboys deranged, models deposed, tree surgeons debarked and dry cleaners depressed?

12. If Fed Ex and UPS were merged, would they call if Fed UP?

13. Do Lipton Tea employees take coffee breaks?

14. What hair color do they put on the driver's license of bald men?

15. I was thinking about how people seem to read the Bible a whole lot more as they get older. Then it dawned on me, they're cramming for their final exam.

16. I thought about how mothers feed their babies with tiny little spoons and forks, so I wondered what do Chinese mothers use - toothpicks?

17. Why do they put pictures of criminals up in the Post Office? What are we supposed to do, write to them? Why don't they just put their pictures on the postage stamps so the mailman can look for them while delivering mail?

18. If it's true that we are here to help others, then what exactly are the others here for?

19. You never really learn to swear until you learn to drive.

20. Ever wonder what the speed of lightning would be if it didn't zigzag?
21. If a cow laughed, would milk come out of her nose?
22. Whatever happened to Preparations A through G?
23. As income tax time approaches, did you ever notice when you put the two words **'The'** and **'IRS'** together it spells **'THEIRS'**?

MOTIVATIONAL POSTERS

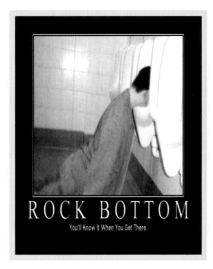

Rules of Man

- Because I'm a man, when I lock my keys in the car, I will fiddle with a coat hanger long after hypothermia has set in. Calling AAA is not an option. I will win.
- Because I'm a man, when the car isn't running very well, I will pop the hood and stare at the engine as if I know what I'm looking at. If another man shows up, one of us will say to the other, "I used to be able to fix these things, but now, with all these computers and everything, I wouldn't know where to start." We will then drink a couple of beers and break wind, as a form of friendship.
- Because I'm a man, when I catch a cold, I need someone to bring me soup and take care of me while I lie in bed and moan. You never get as sick as I do, so for you, this is no problem.
- Because I'm a man, when one of our appliances stops working, I will insist on taking it apart, despite evidence that this will just cost me twice as much once the repair person gets here and has to put it back together.
- Because I'm a man, there is no need to ask me what I'm thinking about. The true answer is always either sex, cars, sex, sports or sex. I have to make up something else when you ask, so don't ask.
- Because I'm a man, I do not want to visit your mother or have your mother come visit us or talk to her when she calls or think about her any more than I have to. Whatever you got her for Mother's Day is okay. I don't need to see it and don't forget to pick up something for my mom, too.
- Because I'm a man, you don't have to ask me if I liked the movie. Chances are, if you're crying at the end of it, I didn't. And if you are feeling amorous afterwards, then I will certainly at least remember the name and recommend it to others.
- Because I'm a man, I think what you're wearing is fine. I thought what you were wearing five minutes ago was fine, too. Either pair of shoes is fine. With the belt or without looks fine. Your hair is fine. You look fine. Can we just go now?
- Because I'm a man, and this is, after all, the year 2007, I will share equally in the housework. You just do the laundry, the cooking, the cleaning, the vacuuming, the dishes, and I'll do the rest; like walking around in the garden with a beer wondering what to do next.

MEN ARE LIKE . . . (thank you Mary)

1. Men are like .....**Laxatives**..... They irritate the crap out of you.
2. Men are like.....**Bananas**..... The older they get, the less firm they are.
3. Men are like .....Weather..... Nothing can be done to change them.
4. Men are like .....**Blenders**..... You need one, but you're not quite sure why.
5. Men are like .....**Chocolate Bars**..... Sweet and smooth and they usually head right for your hips.
6. Men are like .....**Commercials**..... You can't believe a word they say.
7. Men are like .....Department Stores..... Their clothes are always 1/2 off.
8. Men are like .....Government Bonds..... They take soooooooo long to mature.
9. Men are like .....Mascara..... They usually run at the first sign of emotion.
10. Men are like .....Popcorn..... They satisfy you, but only for a little while.
11. Men are like ..... **Snowstorms**..... You never know when they're coming, how many inches you'll get or how long it will last.
12. Men are like .....Lava Lamps ..... Fun to look at, but not very bright.
13. Men are like .....**Parking Spots**..... All the good ones are taken and the rest are handicapped.

PROUD TO BE WHITE

There are African Americans, Mexican Americans, Asian Americans, Arab Americans, Native Americans and so on. Then there are just Americans. You pass me on the street and sneer in my direction. You call me white boy, cracker, honkey, whitey, caveman, etc. and that's OK. But when I call you n*****, towel head, sand-n*****, camel jockey, beaner, gook, chink, etc. you call me a racist.

You have the United Negro College Fund, Martin Luther King Day, Black History Month, Cesar Chavez Day, Ma'uled Al-Nabi, the NAACP and you have BET. If we had WET (White Entertainment Television), we'd be racists. We have a Hispanic Chamber of Commerce, a Black Chamber of Commerce and then we just have the plain Chamber of Commerce. Who pays for that? If we had a college fund that only gave white students scholarships you *know* we'd be racists. There are over 50 openly proclaimed Black-Only Colleges in the USA, yet if there were White-Only Colleges that would be a racist college.

In the Million Man March, you believed that you were marching for your race and rights. If we marched for our race and rights, you would call us racists. You are proud to be black, brown, yellow, orange, etc. and you are not afraid to announce it. But when we announce our white pride, you call us racists. You say that whites commit a lot of violence against you, so why are the ghettos the most dangerous places to live? You rob us, carjack us and shoot at us. But when a white police officer shoots a black gang member or beats up a black drug-dealer who is running from the law and posing a threat to all of society, you call him a racist.

I am proud, **yet you call me a racist**. Why is it that **only whites can be racists?**

Respect the Disadvantaged

Pursue Achievable Goals

NORTH CAROLINA KIN FOLK

Two good ol' boys, Bob and Louis, in a North Carolina trailer park were sitting around talking one afternoon over a cold beer. After a while Bob says to the Louis, "If'n I was to sneak over to your trailer Saturday and make love to your wife while you was off huntin' and she got pregnant and had a baby, would that make us kin?" Louis crooked his head sideways for a minute, scratched his head and squinted his eyes thinking real hard about the question. Finally Louis said to Bob, **"Well, I don't know about kin, but it sure would make us even."**

PHOTOS - BABIES

SMILES BEGIN BECAUSE OF OTHER SMILES

FIND TIME TO RELAX

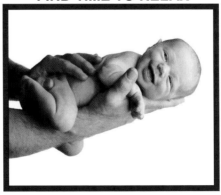

Red Skelton's Recipe for a Good Marriage

- Two times a week we go to a nice restaurant, have a little beverage, good food and companionship. She goes on Tuesdays; I go on Fridays.
- We also sleep in separate beds. Her's is in California and mine is in Texas.
- I take my wife everywhere but she keeps finding her way back.

- I asked my wife where she wanted to go for our anniversary. "Somewhere I haven't been in a long time," she said. So I suggested the kitchen.
- We always hold hands. If I let go, she shops.
- She has an electric blender, electric toaster and electric bread maker. She said "There are too many gadgets and no place to sit down." So I bought her an electric chair.
- My wife told me the car wasn't running well as there was water in the carburetor. I asked, "Where is the car." She told me, "In the lake."
- She got a mud pack and looked great for two days. Then the mud fell off.
- She ran after the garbage truck, yelling, "Am I too late for the garbage?" The driver said, "No, jump in!"
- Remember: Marriage is the number one cause of divorce.
- I married Miss Right. I just didn't know her first name was *Always*.
- I haven't spoken to my wife in 18 months. I don't like to interrupt her.
- The last fight was my fault. My wife asked, "What's on the TV?" I said, "Dust!"

Photos - Boys Will Be Boys and So Will Men

REFLECTIONS - NICE THOUGHTS

I would rather have one rose and a kind word from a friend while I'm here, than a whole truck load when I'm gone.

 Happiness keeps you sweet; Trials keep you strong; Sorrows keep you human; Failures keep you humble; Success keeps you glowing and only You keep you going! Be kinder than necessary, for everyone there is a cross to bear.

VIRUS ALERT

There is a dangerous virus being passed around electronically, orally and by hand. The virus is called Weary-Overload-Recreational-Killer (WORK). If you receive WORK from any of your colleagues, your boss or anyone else via any means, DO NOT TOUCH IT!!! This virus will completely wipe out your private life. If you should come into contact with WORK, put your jacket on and take two good friends to the nearest grocery store. Purchase the antidote known as Work-Isolating-Neutralizer-Extract (WINE)...my personal favorite...ha! Or Bothersome-Employer-Elimination-Rebooter (BEER), take the antidote repeatedly until WORK has been completely eliminated from your system.

MEXICO EARTHQUAKE

A big earthquake, with the strength of 8.1 on the Richter scale, has hit Mexico. Two million Mexicans have died and over a million are injured. The country is totally ruined and the government doesn't know where to start to rebuild. The rest of the world is in shock. Canada is sending troops to help the Mexican army control the riots. Saudi Arabia is sending oil. Other Latin American countries are sending supplies. The European community, except France, is sending food and money.

The United States, not to be outdone, **is sending two million replacement Mexicans.**

58

Signs - BEFORE YOU NAME SOMETHING, T H I N K

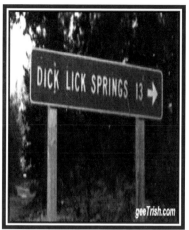

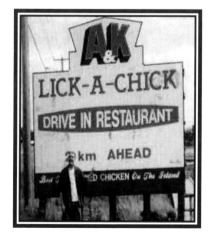

LOVE THOSE ITALIANS

A Greek and an Italian were sitting in a Starbuck's one day discussing who had the superior culture. After triple lattes the Greek guy says, "Well, we have the Parthenon." Arching his eyebrows, the Italian replies, "We have the Coliseum." The Greek retorts, "We Greeks gave birth to advanced mathematics." The Italian, nodding in agreement says, "But we built the Roman Empire." And so on until the Greek comes up with what he thinks will end the discussion. With a flourish of finality he says, "We invented sex!" The Italian replies, "That is true, but it was the Italians who introduced it to women."

VALUABLE RESEARCH INFORMATION: Water - Wine

As Ben Franklin said, "In wine there is wisdom, in beer there is freedom, in water there is bacteria." In a number of carefully controlled trials, scientists have demonstrated that if we drink 1 liter of water each day, at the end of the year we would have absorbed more than 1 kilo of Escherichia Coli (e-coli) bacteria found in feces. In other words we are consuming 1 kilo of poop. However, we do not run that risk when drinking wine and beer (or tequila, rum, whiskey or other hard liquors) because alcohol has to go through a purification process of boiling, filtering and/or fermenting.

Remember: Water = Poop; Wine = Health.

Therefore, it is better to drink wine and talk stupid than to drink water and be full of s***.

BEER vs MAKEUP

She told me we couldn't afford beer anymore and I'd have to quit.
Then I caught her spending $65 on makeup.
And I asked how come I had to give up stuff and she didn't.
She said she needed the makeup to look pretty for me.
I told her that was what the beer was for.
I don't think she's coming back...

A DAMN FINE EXPLANATION

A wife came home early and found her husband in their bedroom making love to a very attractive young woman and was somewhat upset. "You are a disrespectful pig!" she cried. "How dare you do this to me - a faithful wife, the mother of your children! I'm leaving you. I want a divorce straight away!" And the husband replied, "Hang on just a minute love, so at least I can tell you what happened." "Fine, go ahead," she sobbed, "but this will be the last words you will say to me!"

And the husband began. . . "Well, I was getting into the car to drive home and this young lady here asked me for a lift. She looked so down and out and defenseless that I took pity on her and let her into the car. I noticed that she was very thin, not well dressed and very dirty. She told me that she hadn't eaten for three days! So in my compassion, I brought her home and warmed up the enchiladas I made for you last night, the ones you wouldn't eat because you're afraid you'll put on weight. The poor thing devoured them in moments.

Since she needed a good clean up I suggested a shower and while she was doing that I noticed her clothes were dirty and full of holes so I threw them away. Then, as she needed clothes, I gave her the designer jeans that you've had for a few years but don't use because you say they are too tight. I also gave her the underwear that was your anniversary present, which you don't use because I don't have good taste. I found the sexy blouse my sister gave you for Christmas that you don't use, just to annoy her, and I also donated those boots you bought at the expensive boutique and don't use because someone at work has the same pair." The husband took a quick breath and continued. . . "She was so grateful for my understanding and help and as I walked her to the door she turned to me with tears in her eyes and said, "Please, do you have anything else that your wife doesn't use?"

61

BRIDGE TO HAWAII

A Biker was riding along a California beach when suddenly the sky clouded above his head and in a booming voice the Lord said, "Because you have tried to be faithful to me in all ways, I will grant you one wish." The biker pulled over and said, "Build a bridge to Hawaii so I can ride over anytime I want." The Lord said, "Your request is materialistic. Think of the enormous challenges for that

kind of undertaking. The supports that would be required to reach the bottom of the Pacific! The concrete and steel it would take! It will nearly exhaust several natural resources. I can do it, but it is hard for me to justify your desire for worldly things.

Take a little more time and think of something that would honor and glorify me." The biker thought about it for a long time. Finally he said, "Lord, I wish that I could understand my wife. I want to know how she feels inside, what she's thinking when she gives me the silent treatment, why she cries, what she means when she says 'nothing's wrong' and how I can make a woman truly happy."

The Lord replied, **"You want two or four lanes on that bridge?"**

NUCLEAR POWER

Eric was seated next to a little girl on an airplane when the he turned to her and said, "Let's talk. I've heard that flights go quicker if you strike up a conversation with your fellow passenger." The little girl, who had just opened her book, closed it slowly and said to the stranger, "What would you like to talk about?" Oh, I don't know, Eric said. "How about nuclear power?" "OK," she said, "that could be an interesting topic. But let me ask you a question first. A horse, a cow and a deer all eat grass, the same stuff. Yet a deer excretes little pellets, while a cow turns out a flat patty and a horse produces clumps of dried grass. Why do you suppose that is?" Eric thinks about it and says, "Hmmm, I have no idea." To which the little girl replies, "Do you really feel qualified to discuss nuclear power **when you don't know s***?"**

No SEX TONIGHT

I never quite figured out why the sexual urge of men and women differ so much and I never have figured out the whole Venus and Mars thing. I have never figured out why men think with their head and women with their heart.

FOR EXAMPLE: One evening last week my wife and I were getting into bed. Well, the passion starts to heat up and she eventually says, "I don't feel like it. I just want you to hold me." I said, "WHAT? What was that?" So she says the words that every man on the planet dreads to hear: "You're just not in touch with my emotional needs as a woman enough for me to satisfy your physical needs as a man." She responded to my puzzled look by saying, "Can't you just love me for who I am and not what I do for you in the bedroom?" Realizing that nothing was going to happen that night, I went to sleep.

The very next day I opted to take the day off from work to spend time with her. We went out to a nice lunch and then went shopping at a big department store. I walked around with her while she tried on several different expensive outfits. She couldn't decide which one to take so I told her we'd just buy them all. She wanted new shoes to compliment her new clothes so I said, "Lets get a pair for each outfit." We went to the jewelry department where she picked out a pair of diamond earrings. Let me tell you, she was so excited. She must have thought I was one wave short of a shipwreck. I started to think she was testing me because she asked for a tennis bracelet, when she doesn't even know how to play tennis. I think I threw her a loop when I said, "That's fine, honey." She was almost nearing sexual satisfaction from all of the excitement.

Smiling with excited anticipation she finally said, "I think this is all dear, let's go to the cashier." I could hardly contain myself when I blurted out, "No honey, I don't feel like it." Her face just went completely blank as her jaw dropped with a baffled, "WHAT?" I then said, "Honey, I just want you to hold this stuff for a while. You are just not in touch with my financial needs as a man enough for me to satisfy your shopping needs as a woman." And just when she had this look like she was going to kill me, I added, "Why can't you just love me for who I am and not for the things I buy you?"

Apparently, I am not having sex tonight either.

63

PHOTOS - SPORTS PICTURES

The BUCK stops here!

STRESS RELIEF

Just in case you've had a rough day, here's a seven-step stress management technique recommended in the latest psychological texts. The funny thing is, is that it really works.

1. Picture yourself near a stream.
2. Birds are softly chirping in the cool mountain air.
3. No one but you knows your secret place.
4. You are in total seclusion from the hectic world.
5. The soothing sound of a gentle waterfall fills the air with a cascade of serenity.
6. The water is crystal clear.
7. You can easily make out the face of the person you're holding underwater... Feel better?

PHOTOS - SANTA'S HELPER

(Okay, Gwen, we're on a roll now ! bjm).

CHAPTER 3

TWO TOUGH QUESTIONS

If you knew a woman who was pregnant, who had 8 kids already, three who were deaf, two who were blind, one mentally retarded and she had syphilis, would you recommend that she have an abortion? Read the next question before looking at the response for this one. It is time to elect a new world leader and only your vote counts. Here are the facts about the three candidates. Who would you vote for?

Candidate A) Associates with crooked politicians and consults with an astrologist. He's had two mistresses. He also chain smokes and drinks 8 to 10 martinis every day.

Candidate B) He was kicked out of office twice, sleeps until noon, used opium in college and drinks a quart of whiskey every evening.

Candidate C) He is a decorated war hero. He's a vegetarian, doesn't smoke, drinks an occasional beer and never cheated on his wife. Which of these candidates would be your choice? Decide first before looking at the following responses.

Candidate A) is Franklin D. Roosevelt, Candidate B) is Winston Churchill and Candidate C) is Adolph Hitler.

And, by the way, on your answer to the abortion question: If you said YES, you just killed Beethoven. Pretty interesting isn't it? Makes a person think before judging someone. Wait until you see the end of this...Never be afraid to try something new. Remember: Amateurs built the Ark. Professionals built the Titanic.

And finally, can you imagine working for a company that has a little more than 500 employees and has the following statistics: 29 have been accused of spousal abuse, 7 have been arrested for fraud, 19 have been accused of writing bad checks, 117 have directly or indirectly bankrupted at least 2 businesses, 3 have done time for assault, 71 cannot get a credit card due to bad credit, 14 have been arrested on drug-related charges, 8 have been arrested for shoplifting, 21 are currently defendants in lawsuits and 84 have been arrested for drunk driving in the last year... Can you guess which organization this is???

It's the 535 members of the United States Congress. The same group that cranks out hundreds of new laws each year designed to keep the rest of us in line.

68

CARTOONS - THE BEST HOLIDAY HUMOR

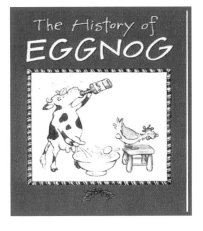

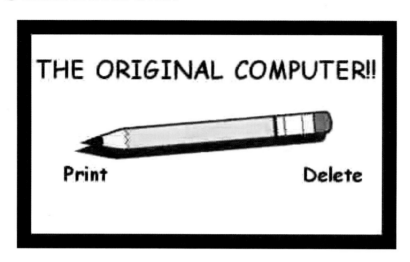

THE ORIGINAL COMPUTER!!

Print   Delete

REMEMBER - LIKE A DUCK

Calm and unruffled on the surface; paddle like the
devil underneath
Be surprised, like you were born yesterday
Live like it is Heaven on Earth
Work as if you did not have to work
Love as if you have never been hurt
Dance as if no one is watching

I WANT IT ON TIME

"I want it on time and in the proper hands. I want it done
correctly, accurately, exactly, precisely, perfectly, efficiently,
reliably, expertly, proficiently, faithfully, totally, absolutely,
unequivocally, unmitigatedly, maturely, flawlessly, supremely,
unsurpassedly and certainly without fault. I want it unharmed,
unbotched, untainted and not screwed-up. And most of all, I want
it done **CHEAP!**"

WORLDS THINNEST BOOKS

- French War Heroes   by Jacques Chirac
- Things I Love About My Country   by Jane Fonda & Cindy Sheehan, (illustrated by Michael Moore)
- My Beauty Secrets   by Janet Reno & Whoopi Goldberg
- All The Women I Have Loved Before   by Barney Frank (D-Mass) & Boy George
- My Christian Accomplishments and How I helped After Katrina   by Rev. Jesse Jackson and Rev. Al Sharpton
- Things I Love About Bill   by Hillary Clinton
- My Little Book of Personal Hygiene   by Osama Bin Laden
- Things I Cannot Afford   by Bill Gates
- Things I Would Not Do for Money   by Dennis Rodman
- Things I Know to be True   by Al Gore and John Kerry
- Amelia Earhart's Guide to the Pacific   by Amelia Earhart
- Collection of Motivational Speeches   by Dr. J. Kevorkian
- All the Men I have Loved Before   by Ellen de Generes & Rosie O'Donnell
- The Guide to Dating Etiquette   by Mike Tyson
- Delicious Spotted Owl Recipes   by PETA
- My Plan to Find The Real Killers   by O.J Simpson
- How to Drink & Drive Over Bridges   by Ted Kennedy
- My Book of Morals   by Bill Clinton (intro by The Rev. Jesse Jackson)

KING ARTHUR AND THE WITCH

Young King Arthur was ambushed and imprisoned by the monarch of a neighboring kingdom. The monarch could have killed him, but was moved by Arthur's youth and ideals. So the monarch offered him his freedom as long as he could answer a very difficult question. Arthur would have a year to figure out the answer and, if after that year, he still had no answer, he would be put to death. The question: **What do women really want?**

Such a question would perplex even the most knowledgeable man, and to young Arthur, it seemed an impossible query. But since it was better than death, he accepted the monarch's proposition to have an answer by year's end. He returned to his kingdom and began to poll everyone; the princess, the priests, the wise men and even the court jester. He spoke with everyone, but no one could give him a satisfactory answer. Many people advised him to consult the old witch, for only she would have the answer. But the prince would be high, as the witch was famous throughout the kingdom for the exorbitant prices she charged.

The last day of the year arrived and Arthur had no choice but to talk to the witch. She agreed to answer the question, but he would have to agree to her price first. The old witch wanted to marry Sir Lancelot, the most noble of the Knights of the Round Table and Arthur's closest friend. Young Arthur was horrified. She was hunchbacked and hideous, had only one tooth, smelled like sewage, made obscene noises, etc. He had never encountered such a repugnant creature in all his life. He refused to force his friend to marry her and endure such a terrible burden, but Lancelot, learning of the proposal, spoke with Arthur.

He said nothing was too big a sacrifice compared to Arthur's life and the preservation of the Round Table. Hence, a wedding was proclaimed and the witch answered Arthur's question, thus: "What a woman really wants," she answered, "is to be in charge of her own life." Everyone in the kingdom instantly knew that the witch had uttered a great truth and that Arthur's life would be spared. And so it was, the neighboring monarch granted Arthur his freedom and Lancelot and the witch had a wonderful wedding.

The honeymoon hour approached and Lancelot, steadying himself for a horrific experience, entered the bedroom; but what a sight awaited him. The most beautiful woman he had ever seen lay before him on the bed. The astounded Lancelot asked, "What happened?" The beauty replied that since he had been so kind to her when she appeared as the witch, she would henceforth, be her horrible deformed self only half the time and the beautiful maiden the other half. "Which would you prefer? Beautiful during the day or night?" she asked. Lancelot pondered the predicament. During the day, a beautiful woman to show off to his friends, but at night, in the privacy of his castle, an old witch? Or, would he prefer having a hideous witch during the day, but by night, a beautiful woman for him to enjoy wondrous intimate moments?

What would YOU do? What Lancelot chose is below. BUT, make YOUR choice before you look OK? Nobel Lancelot said that he would **allow HER to make the choice herself.** Upon hearing this, she announced that she would be beautiful all the time because he had respected her enough to let her be in charge of her own life. Now, what's the moral of this story?

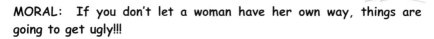

MORAL: If you don't let a woman have her own way, things are going to get ugly!!!

CARTOONS - SILLY

OK, So we've taken off our clothes and I'm on top of you - how long before we get that orgasm thing?

I don't know but now I understand why mummy has a headache all the time!

HISTORY - LIBERALS and CONSERVATIVE

Humans originally existed as members of small bands of nomadic hunters/gatherers. They lived on deer in the mountains during the summer and would go to the coast and live on fish and lobster in the winter. The two most important events in all of history were the invention of beer and the invention of the wheel. The wheel was invented to get man to the beer. These were the foundation of modern civilization and together were the catalyst for the splitting of humanity into two distinct subgroups:
1) Liberals and 2) Conservatives.

Once beer was discovered, it required grain and that was the beginning of agriculture. Neither the glass bottle nor aluminum can were invented yet, so while our early humans were sitting around waiting for them to be invented, they just stayed close to the brewery. That's how villages were formed. Some men spent their days tracking and killing animals to BB-Q at night while they were drinking beer. This was the beginning of what is known as the **Conservative** Movement. Other men who were weaker and less skilled at hunting learned to live off the conservatives by showing up for the nightly BB-Q's and doing the sewing, fetching and hair dressing.

This was the beginning of the **Liberal** Movement. Some of these liberal men eventually evolved into women. The rest became known as 'Girly-Men or Wussies'. Some noteworthy liberal achievements include the domestication of cats, the invention of group therapy, group hugs and the concept of voting to decide how to divide the meat and beer that conservatives provided.

Over the years **Conservatives** came to be symbolized by the largest, most powerful land animal on earth; the elephant. **Liberals** are symbolized by the jackass. A few modern liberals like Mexican light beer (with lime added), but most prefer a chilled glass of Sauvignon Blanc with passion fruit and kiwi aromas which are marked by grassy notes then rounded out on the mid palate by peach flavors. Crisp and refreshing with a hint of chalky minerality on the finish or Perrier bottled water. They eat raw fish but dislike beef. Sushi, tofu, and French food are standard liberal fare.

Another interesting evolutionary side note: most **Liberal** women have higher testosterone levels than their men. Most social workers, personal injury attorneys, Ivy League professors, journalists, dreamers in Hollywood and group therapists are liberals. Liberals invented the designated-hitter rule because it wasn't fair to make the pitcher also bat.

Conservatives drink Sam Adams, Harpoon IPA or Yuengling Lager. They eat red meat and still provide for their women. Conservatives are big-game hunters, rodeo cowboys, lumberjacks, construction workers, firemen, medical doctors, police officers, corporate executives, athletes, Marines, and generally anyone who works productively. Conservatives, who own companies, hire other conservatives who want to work for a living. Liberals produce little or nothing. They like to govern the producers and decide what to do with the production. **Liberals** believe Europeans are more enlightened than Americans. That is why most of the Liberals remained in Europe when Conservatives were coming to America. They crept in after the Wild West was tamed and created a business of trying to get more for nothing.

Here ends today's lesson in world history: It should be noted that a **Liberal** may have a momentary urge to angrily respond to the above before forwarding it. A **Conservative** will simply laugh and be so convinced of the absolute truth of this history that it will be forwarded immediately to other true believers and to more Liberals just to piss them off.

Photos - SANTA'S SLEIGH

ANNIVERSARY GIFT

He forgot his wedding anniversary. His wife was really angry. She told him, "Tomorrow morning, I expect to find a gift in the driveway that goes from 0 to 200 in 6 seconds AND IT BETTER BE THERE!!" The next morning, Bob got up early and left for work. When his wife woke up, she looked out the window and sure enough there was a box gift-wrapped in the middle of the driveway. Confused, the wife put on her robe and ran out to the driveway and brought the box into the house. She opened it and found a brand new bathroom scale. **Bob has been missing since Friday...**

SENILE LIKE A FOX

One sunny day in 2008, an old man approached the White House from across Pennsylvania Avenue, where he'd been sitting on a park bench. He spoke to the Marine standing guard and said, "I would like to go in and meet with President Hillary Clinton." The Marine replied, "Sir, Mrs. Clinton is not President and doesn't reside here." The old man said, "Okay," and walked away. The following day, the same man approached the White House and said to the same Marine, "I would like to go in and meet with President Hillary Clinton." The Marine again told the man, "Sir, as I said yesterday, Mrs. Clinton is not the President and doesn't reside here." The man thanked him and again walked away. The third day, the same man approached the White House and spoke to the very same Marine, saying, "I would like to go in and meet with President Hillary Clinton." The Marine, understandably agitated at this point, looked at the man and said, "Sir, this is the third day in a row you have been here asking to speak to Mrs. Clinton. I've told you already several times that **Mrs. Clinton is not the President and doesn't reside here.** Don't you understand?" The old man answered, "Oh, I understand you fine. I just love hearing your answer!" The Marine snapped to attention, saluted and said, "See you tomorrow!"

76

Rules FOR BEDROOM GOLF (Dedicated to Doris)

1. Each player shall furnish his own equipment for play, normally one club and two balls.

2. Play on a course must be approved by the owner of the hole.

3. Unlike outdoor golf, the object is to get the club in the hole and keep the balls out of the hole.

4. For most effective play, the club should have a firm shaft. Course owners are permitted to check the shaft stiffness before play begins.

5. Course owners reserve the right to restrict the length of the club to avoid damage to the hole.

6. The object of the game is to take as many strokes as necessary until the course owner is satisfied the play is complete. Failure to do so may result in being denied permission to play the course again.

7. It is considered bad form to begin playing the hole immediately upon arrival at the course. The experienced player will normally take time to admire the entire course with special attention to well formed bunkers.

8. Players are cautioned not to mention other courses they have played or are currently playing to the owner of the course being played. Upset course owners have been known to damage a player's equipment for this reason.

9. Players are encouraged to have proper rain gear along, just in case.

10. Players should assure themselves that their match has been properly scheduled, particularly when a new course is being played for the first time. Previous players have been known to become irate if they discover someone else playing what they consider to be a private course.

QUESTIONNAIRE - COMPLETE QUESTIONS IN LEFT COLUMN TO HELP PREPARE A LETTER TO SANTA CLAUS. COMPLETED SAMPLE LETTER NEXT PAGE (THIS IS FOR BIG GIRLS AND BOYS).

QUESTIONS	ANSWERS (these are Billie's answers)
Girl or Boy	Girl
Friend's Name	Bella
Another Friend's Name	John
Drink	Champagne
Number	7
Scent or Odor	Lemons
Friend's Name	Gwenie
Article of Clothing	Bra
Dance	Dirty
Furniture	Sofa
Song Title	You've Lost that Lovin' Feeling
Electronic Device	Vibrator
Crime	Rape
Married Male Friend	Keith
Adjective	Little
Farm Animal	Pig
Color	Black
Another Color	Red
Married Female Friend	Jeannie
Body Part	Genitals
Food	Caviar
Vehicle	Sleigh
Part of a House	Bedroom
Adjective	Disgusting
Animal	Bitch
Crime	Sexual Exposure
Adjective	Dirty
Adjective	Smelly
Adjective	Naughty
Adverb	Soooooo
Your Name	Billie Jo
Number	313

QUESTIONNAIRE LETTER TO SANTA CLAUSE FROM BIG GIRLS AND BOYS

TO: Santa Claus, North Pole, Earth

Dear Santa:
I have been a good GIRL.

It really wasn't my fault what happened at BELLA's office party. It was JOHN who spiked the punch with too much CHAMPAGNE. I can't help it if I drank 7 glasses. It was so good -- smelled and tasted just like LEMONS.

I thought it was funny when I put GWENIE's BRA on my head and danced the DIRTY on the SOFA while singing 'YOU'VE LOST THAT LOVIN FEELIN'. I didn't mean to break BELLA's VIBRATOR and don't know why BELLA would accuse me of RAPE.

I don't remember calling KEITH's wife a LITTLE PIG -- even though she looked like one with BLACK eye shadow and RED lipstick!

And when I threw up on JEANNIE'S husband's GENITALS, it was only because I ate too much of that CAVIAR.

After all that fun, I admit I was a little tired. So I fell asleep on my way home and drove my SLEIGH through my neighbor's BEDROOM. I don't think that was any reason for my neighbor to call me a DISGUSTING BITCH and have me arrested for SEXUAL EXPOSURE!

So Santa, here I sit in my jail cell on Christmas Eve all DIRTY and SMELLY. And I'm really not to blame for any of this NAUGHTY stuff. Please bring me what I want the most -- bail money!

Sincerely and SOOOOO yours,
BILLIE JO (Really a nice GIRL!)

P.S. It's only $313 bucks!

79

COKE OR WATER?

WATER:

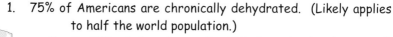

1. 75% of Americans are chronically dehydrated. (Likely applies to half the world population.)
2. In 37% of Americans, the thirst mechanism is so weak that it is mistaken for hunger.
3. Even MILD dehydration will slow down one's metabolism as much as 3%
4. One glass of water will shut down midnight hunger pangs for almost 100% of the dieters studied in a University of Washington study.
5. Lack of water, the #1 trigger of daytime fatigue.
6. Preliminary research indicates that 8-10 glasses of water a day could significantly ease back and joint pain for up to 80% of sufferers.
7. A mere 2% drop in body water can trigger fuzzy short-term memory trouble with basic math and difficulty focusing on the computer screen or on a printed page.
8. Drinking 5 glasses of water daily decreases the risk of colon cancer by 45%, plus it can slash the risk of breast cancer by 79% and one is 50% less likely to develop bladder cancer.

Are you drinking the amount of water you should drink every day?

COKE:

1. In many states the highway patrol carries two gallons of Coke in the trunk to remove blood from the highway after a car accident.
2. You can put a T-bone steak in a bowl of Coke and it will be gone in two days.
3. To clean a toilet: Pour a can of Coca-Cola into the toilet bowl and let the 'real thing' sit for one hour, then flush clean. The citric acid in Coke removes stains from vitreous china.
4. To remove rust spots from chrome car bumpers: Rub the bumper with a rumpled-up piece of Reynolds Wrap aluminum foil dipped in Coca-Cola.
5. To clean corrosion from car battery terminals: Pour a can of Coca-Cola over the terminals to bubble away the corrosion.
6. To loosen a rusted bolt: Apply a cloth soaked in Coca-Cola to the rusted bolt for several minutes.

7. To bake a moist ham: Empty a can of Coke into the baking pan, wrap the ham in aluminum foil and bake. Thirty minutes before ham is finished, remove the foil, allowing the drippings to mix with the Coke for a sumptuous brown gravy.

8. To remove grease from clothes: Empty a can of Coke into the load of greasy clothes, add detergent and run through a regular cycle. The Coca-Cola will help loosen grease stains. It will also clean road haze from your windshield.

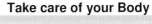

FOR YOUR INFORMATION:

1. The active ingredient in Coke is phosphoric acid. It will dissolve a nail in about four days. Phosphoric acid also leaches calcium from bones and is a major contributor to the rising increase of osteoporosis.

2. To carry Coca-Cola syrup, the concentrate, the commercial trucks must use a hazardous material place card reserved for highly corrosive materials.

3. The distributors of Coke have been using it to clean the engines of their trucks for about 20 years!

Now, the question is, would you like a glass of water or Coke?

PHOTOS - MORE BABIES!

| **Take care of your Friends** | **Take care of your Body** |

MARKETING 101
Understanding Practical Marketing 101

The buzz word in today's business world is **MARKETING**. However, people often ask for a simple explanation of 'Marketing'. Well, here it is:

1. You're a woman and you see a handsome guy at a party. You go up to him and say, "I'm fantastic in bed." **That's Direct Marketing**

2. You're at a party with a bunch of friends and see a handsome guy. One of your friends goes up to him and, pointing at you, says, "She's fantastic in bed." **That's Advertising**

3. You see a handsome guy at a party. You go up to him and get his telephone number. The next day you call and say, "Hi, I'm fantastic in bed." **That's Telemarketing**

4. You see a guy at a party; you straighten your dress. You walk up to him and pour him a drink. You say, "May I, as you reach up to straighten his tie, brushing your breast lightly against his arm, and then say, "By the way, I'm fantastic in bed." **That's Public Relations**

5. You're at a party and see a handsome guy. He walks up to you and says, "I hear you're fantastic in bed." **That's Brand Recognition**

6. You're at a party and see a handsome guy. He fancies you, but you talk him into going home with your friend. **That's a Sales Rep**

7. Your friend can't satisfy him so he calls you. **That's Tech Support**

8. You're on your way to a party when you realize that there could be handsome men in all these houses you're passing, so you climb onto the roof of one situated towards the center and shout at the top of your lungs, "I'm fantastic in bed!" **That's Junk Mail**

9. You're at a party; this well-built man walks up to you and grabs your ass. **That's the Governor of California**

10. You like it, but twenty years later your attorney decides you were offended. **THAT'S AMERICA...**

Photos - amusing

BLOCK YOUR DRIVER'S LICENSE

This is upsetting so I thought I should pass it along. Now you can see anyone's driver's license on the internet, including your own! I just searched for mine and there it was... Thanks Homeland Security! I definitely removed mine and I suggest you all do the same. Go to the website and check it out. Just enter your name, City and State to see if you're on file. After your license comes on the screen, click the box marked 'Please Remove'. This will remove it from public viewing but not from law enforcement. I promptly did exactly what I was told to do by Billie Jo and look at what came up:

MILKING MACHINE

A farmer ordered a high-tech milking machine. Since the equipment arrived, when his wife was out of town, he decided to test it on himself first. So he inserted his 'manhood' into the equipment, turned on the switch and everything else was automatic. Soon, he realized that the equipment provided him with much more pleasure than his wife did. When the fun was over though, he quickly realized that he couldn't remove the instrument from his 'member'. He read the manual but didn't find any useful information on how to disengage himself. He tried every button on the instrument, but still without success. Finally, he decided to call the supplier's Customer Service Hot Line with his cell phone (thank God for cell phones!). "Hello, I just bought a milking machine from your company. It works fantastic, but how do I remove it from the cow's utter?" "Don't worry," replied the customer service rep, "the machine will release automatically once it's collected **two gallons**. Have a nice day..."

A GOOD HUSBAND

Jack wakes up with a huge hangover after the night at a business function. He forces himself to open his eyes and the first thing he sees is a couple of aspirins next to a glass of water on the side table. And next to them, a single red rose! Jack sits up and sees his clothing in front of him, all cleaned and pressed. Jack looks around the room and sees that it is in perfect order, spotlessly clean. So is the rest of the house. He takes the aspirins, cringes when he sees a huge black eye staring back at him in the bathroom mirror and notices a note on the table: "Honey, breakfast is on the stove, I left early to go shopping. Love you!" He stumbles to the kitchen and sure enough, there is hot breakfast and the morning newspaper. His son is also at the table, eating. Jack asks, "Son, what happened last night?" "Well, you came home after 3 am, drunk and out of your mind. You broke the coffee table, puked in the hallway and got that black eye when you ran into the door." "So, why is everything in such perfect order, so clean, I have a rose and breakfast is on the table waiting for me?" His son replies, "Oh, THAT! Mom dragged you to the bedroom and when she tried to take your pants off you screamed, "Leave me alone, bitch, I'm married!"

Broken table - $200	Red Rose bud - $3
Hot breakfast - $5	Two aspirins - $0.25

Saying the right thing at the right time... Priceless

PHOTOS - WHEN NOT TO POSE

The Breast Stroke	Tent City

85

WOMAN'S PIERCING - THE ULTIMATE MAN'S VIEW

Men all over the country are urging their wives and sweethearts to get this 'chic' procedure. The going rate on the East coast now exceeds $10,000. Many men feel it's worth it.

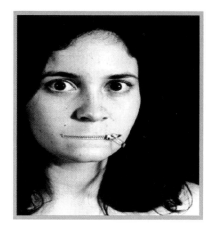

SORRY - I DON'T HAVE MONEY!

Dear Sweetheart, I can't send my salary this month, so I am sending 100 kisses. You are my sweetheart,   **Your Husband**

His wife replied back after some days:

My Darling, Thanks for your 100 kisses, I am sending the expense details.

- The milk man agreed on 2 kisses for one month's milk.
- The electricity man only agreed after 7 kisses.
- Your house owner is coming every day and taking two or three kisses instead of the rent.
- The supermarket owner did not accept kisses only, so I have given him some other items...
- Other expenses 40 kisses.

Please don't worry about me, I have a remaining balance of 35 kisses and I hope I can complete the month using this balance. Shall I plan the same way for next month? Please advise,

Your Sweetheart

BECOMING ILLEGAL

Dear Assemblyman Burton:

As a native Californian and excellent customer of the IRS, I am writing to ask for your assistance. I have contacted the Department of Homeland Security in an effort to determine the process for becoming an illegal alien and they refereed me to you. My primary reason for wishing to change my status from US Citizen to illegal alien stems from the bill which was recently passed by the Senate and for which you voted. If my understanding of this bill's provisions is accurate, as an illegal alien who has been in the United States for five years, all I need to do to become a citizen is to pay a $2,000 fine and income taxes for three of the last five years. I know a good deal when I see one and I am anxious to get the process started before everyone figures it out.

Simply put, those of us who have been here legally have had to pay taxes every year so I'm excited about the prospect of avoiding two years of taxes in return for paying a $2,000 fine. Is there any way that I can apply to be illegal retroactively? This would yield an excellent result for me and my family because we paid heavy taxes in 2004 and 2005. Additionally, as an illegal alien I could begin using the local emergency room as my primary health care provider. Once I have stopped paying premiums for medical insurance, my accountant figures I could save almost $10,000 a year. Another benefit in gaining illegal status would be that my daughter would receive preferential treatment relative to school applications, as well as instate tuition rates for many colleges throughout the United States for my son.

Lastly, I understand that Illegal Status would relieve me of the burden of renewing my driver's license and making those burdensome car insurance premiums. This is very important to me given that I still have college-age children driving my car.

If you would provide me with an outline of the process to become illegal (retroactively if possible) and copies of the necessary forms, I would be most appreciative. Thank you for your assistance,

Your Loyal Constituent,
Dave Haskit, CA

YOU KNOW YOU'VE BEEN OUT OF YOUR 20'S WHEN:

Your potted plants stay alive. Having sex in a twin-sized bed is absurd. You keep more food than beer in the fridge. 6:00 am is when you get up, not when you go to sleep. You hear your favorite song on the elevator at work. You carry an umbrella. You watch the Weather Channel. Your friends 'marry and divorce' instead of 'hook-up and break-up'. You go from 130 days of vacation time to 7. Jeans and a sweater no longer qualify as 'dressed up'. You're the one calling the police because the kids next door won't turn down the stereo. Older relatives feel comfortable telling sex jokes around you. You don't know what time Taco Bell closes anymore. Your car insurance goes down and your car payments go up. You no longer take naps from noon to 6 pm. MTV News is no longer your primary source for information. You go to the drugstore for Ibuprofen and antacids, not condoms and pregnancy test kits. A $4.00 bottle of wine is no longer 'pretty good stuff'. You actually eat breakfast foods at breakfast time. Grocery lists are longer than Macaroni & Cheese, Diet Pepsi and Ho-Ho's. "I just can't drink the way I used to," replaces, "I'm never going to drink that much again."

VIAGRA - IRISH

An Irish woman of advanced age visited her physician to ask his help in reviving her husband's libido. "What about trying Viagra?" asked the doctor. "Not a chance," she said, "he won't even take an aspirin." "Not a problem," replied the doctor. "Give him an 'Irish Viagra'. It's when you drop the Viagra tablet into his coffee. He won't even taste it. Give it a try and call me in a week to let me know how things went." It wasn't a week later that she called the doctor, who directly inquired as to the progress. The poor dear exclaimed, "Oh, faith, bejeysus and begorrah! T'was horrid! Just terrible, doctor!" "Really? What happened?" asked the doctor. "Well, I did as you advised and slipped it in his coffee and the effect was almost immediate. He jumped straight up, with a twinkle in his eye and with his pants a-bulging fiercely! With one swoop of his arm, he sent the cups and tablecloth flying, ripped me clothes to tatters and took me then and there, took me passionately on the tabletop! It was a nightmare, I tell you, an absolute nightmare!" "Why so terrible?" asked the doctor, "Do you mean the sex your husband provided wasn't good?" "T'was the best sex I've had in 25 years! But sure as I'm sittin' here, **I'll never be able to show me face in Starbucks again!"**

Are you lonely ???

Don't like working on your own ?
Hate making decisions ?

Then call a MEETING !!

You can ....
SEE people
DRAW flowcharts
FEEL important
FORM subcommittees
IMPRESS your colleagues
MAKE meaningless recommendations
    ALL on COMPANY TIME !!!!

MEETINGS .....

THE PRACTICAL ALTERNATIVE TO WORK.

BULLETIN

This JOB is a test.
It is only a test.
Had it been a actual job,
You would have received
Bonuses, Raises and
Promotions.

RESTROOM USE POLICY

To: All Employees, In the past, employees were permitted to make trips to the restrooms under informal guidelines. Effective October 1, 2004, a restroom trip policy will be established to provide a more consistent method of accounting for each employee's restroom time and to ensure equal treatment of all employees. Under the policy, a 'Restroom Trip Bank' will be established for each employee. The first day of each month, employees will be given twenty (20) Restroom Trip Credits. These credits may be accumulated. Within the next two weeks, the entrances to all restrooms will be equipped with personnel identification stations and computerized voice recognition devices. The voice print recognition stations will be optional but not required for the month of September. Employees should acquaint themselves with the stations during that period. If an employee's Restroom Trip Bank balance reaches zero, the doors to the restrooms will not unlock for that employee's voice until the first of the next month. Employee's using their voice to open the door for others will not be tolerated! In addition, all restroom stalls are being equipped with timed paper roll retractors. If the stall is occupied for more than five minutes, an alarm will sound. Thirty seconds after the alarm sounds, the toilet paper roll will retract into the wall, the toilet will flush and the stall door will open. If the stall remains occupied, your picture will be taken. These pictures will then be posted on the bulletin board. Anyone's picture showing up three times will immediately be terminated.

PHOTOS - A 320 POUND WOMAN

What does a 320 pound woman look like? What were you expecting? The tallest and biggest woman in the world lives in Holland. She is 7'4" and weights 320lbs.

MAXINE - THE BANNISTER OF LIFE

As You Slide Down the Banister of Life Remember...

- Jim Baker and Jimmy Swaggert have written an impressive new book. It's called "Ministers Do More Than Lay People."
- Transvestite: A guy who likes to eat, drink and be Mary.
- The difference between the Pope and your boss: the Pope only expects you to kiss his ring.
- My mind works like lightning. One brilliant flash and it is gone.
- The only time the world beats a path to your door is if you're in the bathroom.
- I hate sex in the movies. Tried it once. The seat folded up, the drink spilled and that ice, well, it really chilled the mood.
- A husband is someone who, after taking the trash out, gives the impression that he just cleaned the whole house.
- My next house will have no kitchen - just vending machines and a large trash can.
- A blonde said, "I was worried that my mechanic might try to rip me off. I was relieved when he told me all I needed was turn signal fluid."
- I'm so depressed. My doctor refused to write me a prescription for Viagra. He said it would be like putting a new flagpole on a condemned building.
- My neighbor was bit by a stray rabid dog. I went to see how he was and found him writing frantically on a piece of paper. I told him rabies could be treated and he didn't have to worry about a Will. He said, "Will? What Will? I'm making a list of people I want to bite."
- Definition of a teenager? God's punishment for enjoying sex.
- As you slide down the banister of life, may the splinters never point the wrong way.

IBM BALL REPLACEMENT

This is an actual alert to IBM Field Engineers that went out to all IBM Branch Officers. The person who wrote it was very serious. The rest of us find it rather funny. Abstract Mouse Balls Available as FRU (Field Replacement Unit). Mouse balls are now available as FRU. Therefore, if a mouse fails to operate or should it perform erratically, it may need a ball replacement. Because of the delicate nature of this procedure, replacement of mouse balls should only be attempted by properly trained personnel. Before proceeding, determine the type of mouse balls by examining the underside of the mouse. Domestic balls will be lighter and harder than foreign balls. Ball removal procedures differ depending upon the manufacturer of the mouse. Foreign balls can be replaced using the twist-off method. Mouse balls are not usually static sensitive. However, excessive handling can result in sudden discharge. Upon completion of ball replacement, the mouse may be used immediately. It is recommended that each replacer have a pair of spare balls for maintaining optimum customer satisfaction and that any customer missing his balls should suspect local personnel of removing these necessary items. To re-order, specify one of the following: Domestic Mouse Balls or Foreign Mouse Balls

SUNBATHING

Mary, who was a rather well-proportioned executive, spent almost all of her vacation sunbathing on the roof of her hotel. She wore a bathing suit the first day, but on the second, she decided that no one could see her way up there so she slipped out of it for an overall tan. She'd hardly begun when she heard someone running up the stairs. She was lying on her stomach, so she just pulled a towel over her rear.

"Excuse me, Mary," said the flustered assistant manager of the hotel, out of breath from running up the stairs. "The Hilton doesn't mind your sunbathing on the roof but we would very much appreciate your wearing a bathing suit as you did yesterday." "What difference does it make?" Mary asked rather calmly. "No one can see me up here, besides I'm covered with a towel." "Not exactly," said the embarrassed man. **"You're lying on the dining room skylight."**

WOMEN - FEELINGS ABOUT BUTT SIZE

There is a new study just released by the American Psychiatric Association about women and how they feel about their asses. The results are pretty interesting:

- 5% of women surveyed feel their ass is too big.
- 10% of women surveyed feel their ass is too small.
- The remaining 85% said they don't care, they love him, he's a good man and they still would have married him!

PHOTOS - THOUGHTS TO LIVE BY

Take Risks

Surf the Net

Teamwork

Share with Others
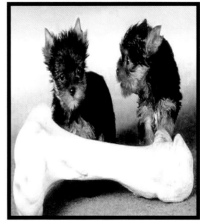

Photos - MORE THOUGHTS TO LIVE BY

Get Along with Others   **Maintain Humor**

Lighten the Atmosphere

Ahhhhhh !!!...

Prescription

Jill walked into her small-town pharmacy and said she wanted to purchase some cyanide. The pharmacist said, "Why in the world do you need cyanide?" Jill then explained she needed it to poison her husband. The pharmacist's eyes got big and he said, "Lord, have mercy. I can't give you cyanide to kill your husband! That's against the law! I'll lose my license, they'll throw both of us in jail and...and all kinds of bad things will happen. Absolutely not, you may NOT have any cyanide!" Then Jill reached into her purse and pulled out a picture of her husband in bed with the pharmacist's wife. The pharmacist looked at the picture and replied, "Well now, you didn't tell me you had a prescription!"

94

PHOTOS - FIRST KISS

EMERGENCY ROOM

The other day Eli needed to go to the emergency room. Not wanting to sit for 4 hours, he put on his old Army fatigues and stuck a patch on that he had downloaded off the internet onto the front of his shirt. When he went into the emergency room he noticed that about 3/4 of the people got up and left. "I guess they decided they weren't that sick after all," Eli thought.

Here's the patch. Feel free to use it the next time you're in need of quicker emergency service.

Story told in 'Love Signs'

(read carefully left to right)

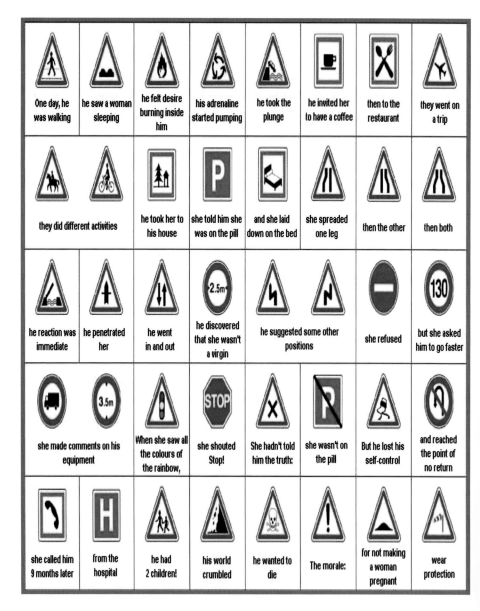

96

CARTOONS - A FRIEND IS LIKE A GOOD BRA #1

A friend is like a good bra: Hard to find, supportive, comfortable, always lifts you up, never lets you down or leaves you hanging and always close to your heart!

VIAGRA - A NEW NAME

In Pharmacology, all drugs have two names, a trade name and a generic name. For example, the trade name of Tylenol also has a generic name of Acetaminophen. Aleve is also called Naproxen. Amoxil is also called Amoxicillin and Advil is also called Ibuprofen. The FDA has been looking for a generic name for Viagra. After careful consideration by a team of government experts, they recently announced that they have settled on the generic name of *Mycoxafloppin*. Also considered were *Mycoxafailin*, *Mydixadrupin*, *Mydixarizin*, *Dixafix*, and of course, *Ibepokin*. Pfizer Corp. announced today that Viagra will soon be available in liquid form and will be marketed by Pepsi Cola as a power beverage suitable for use as a mixer. It will now be possible for a man to literally pour himself a 'stiff one'. Obviously we can no longer call this a 'soft drink' and it gives new meaning to the names of 'cocktails', 'highballs' and just a good old-fashioned 'stiff drink'. Pepsi will market the new concoction by the name of: 'MOUNT & DO'.

Thought for the day: There is more money being spent on breast implants and Viagra today than on Alzheimer's research. This means that by 2040, there should be a large elderly population with perky boobs, huge erections and absolutely no recollection of what to do with them!

PHOTOS - THINGS TO DO WHEN CO-WORKERS ARE ON VACATION

PHOTOS - F I R E D ! !

INTERGALACTIC TRAVEL

Two aliens landed in the Arizona desert near a gas station that was closed for the night. They approached one of the gas pumps and the younger alien addressed it saying, "Greetings, Earthling. We come in peace. Take us to your leader." The gas pump, of course, didn't respond. The younger alien became angry at the lack of response and the older alien said, "I'd calm down if I were you." The younger alien ignored the warning and repeated his greeting. Again there was no response. Annoyed by what he perceived to be the pump's haughty attitude, he drew his ray gun and said impatiently, "Greetings, Earthling. We come in peace. Do not ignore us this way! Take us to your leader or I will fire!"

The older alien warned his comrade saying,  "You don't want to do that! I don't think you should make him mad." "Rubbish," replied the cocky, young alien. He aimed his weapon at the pump and opened fire. There was a huge explosion. A massive fireball roared towards them, blew the younger alien off his feet and deposited him as a burnt, crumpling mess about 200 yards away in a cactus patch. About a half hour passed when he finally regained consciousness. He refocused his three eyes, straightened his bent antenna and looked dazedly at the older, wiser alien who was standing over him shaking his big, green head.

"What a ferocious creature!" exclaimed the young, fried alien. "He damn near killed me! How did you know he was so dangerous?" The older alien leaned over, placed a friendly feeler on his crispy friend and replied, "If there's one thing I've learned during my intergalactic travels, you don't want to mess with a guy who can wrap his penis around himself twice and then stick it in his ear."

OMELET

Today's Ebonics word from the Louisiana Public School System: Omelet

Let's use it in a sentence: "I should pop yo azz fo what you jus did, but omelet dis one slide."

PHOTOS - ARE YOU 'REALLY' READY FOR THIS? (I'm already bored)

THE AISLE SEAT

Two Arabs boarded a flight out of London. One took a window seat and the other one sat next to him in the middle seat. Just before takeoff, a Marine sat down in the aisle seat. After takeoff, the Marine kicked his shoes off, wiggled his toes and was settling in when the Arab in the window seat said, "I need to get up and get a Coke." The Marine said, "Don't get up, I'm in the aisle seat. I'll get it for you." As soon as he left, one of the Arabs picked up the Marine's shoe and spat in it. When the Marine returned with the Coke, the other Arab said, "That looks good, I'd really like one too." Again, the Marine obligingly went to fetch it. While he was gone the other Arab picked up the Marine's other shoe and spat in it. When the Marine returned, they all sat back and enjoyed the flight. As the plane was landing, the Marine slipped his feet into his shoes and knew immediately what had happened. "Why does it have to be this way?" he asked. "How long must this go on? This fighting between our nations? This hatred? This animosity? This spitting in shoes and pissing in Cokes?" THE MARINES WILL ALWAYS WIN.

100

DADDY LONGLEGS

A father watched his young daughter playing in the garden. He smiled as he reflected on how sweet and pure his little girl was. Tears formed in his eyes as he thought about her seeing the wonders of nature through such innocent eyes. Suddenly she just stopped and stared at the ground. He went over to her to see what work of God had captured her attention. He noticed she was looking at two spiders mating. "Daddy, what are those two spiders doing?" she asked. "They're mating," her father replied. "What do you call the spider on top?" she asked. "That's a Daddy Longlegs," her father answered. "So, the other one is a Mommy Longlegs?" the little girl asked. As his heart soared with the joy of such a cute and innocent question he replied, "No dear. Both of them are Daddy Longlegs." The little girl, looking a little puzzled, thought for a moment and then took her foot and stomped them flat. "Well, we're not having any of that gay s*** in our garden!" she said.

U.S. TROOPS ACCUSED OF CHILD ABUSE IN IRAQ

Forced labor by troops

GI attempts to eat Iraqi child

Talk or I'll tickle you 'til you pee

Forces child to hang by fingers

No fire during Soccer game

WORDS WOMEN USE

1. **Fine**: This is the word women use to end an argument when they're right and you need to just shut the hell up.
2. **Five Minutes**: If she is getting dressed, this means half an hour. 'Five minutes' is only 'five minutes' if you have just been given 'five minutes' to watch the game before helping around the house.
3. **Nothing**: This is the calm before the storm. This means something and you should be on your toes. Arguments that begin with 'nothing' usually end in 'fine'.
4. **Go Ahead**: This is a dare, not permission. Don't Do It!!!
5. **Loud Sigh**: This is actually a word but is a non-verbal statement often misunderstood by men. A 'loud sigh' means she wants to think long and hard before deciding how and when you will pay for your mistake.
6. **That's Okay**: This is one of the *most dangerous* statements a woman can make to a man. 'That's okay' means she thinks you're and idiot and wonders why she is wasting her time standing here arguing with you about 'nothing'. (Refer back to #3 for the meaning of 'nothing').
7. **Thanks**: A woman is thanking you, do not question it or faint. Just say, "You're welcome."
8. **Whatever**: Is a woman's way of saying F*** YOU!
9. **Don't worry about it, I got it**: Another dangerous statement, meaning this is something that a woman has told a man to do several times, but is now doing it herself. This will later result in a man asking, "What's wrong?" See #3 above for response...

GO FLY A KITE

A husband is in his backyard trying to fly a kite. He throws the kite up, the wind catches it for a few seconds and then it comes crashing back down. He tries this a few more times with no success. All the while his wife is watching him from the kitchen window, muttering to herself how men need to be told how to do everything. She opens the window and yells to her husband, "You need a piece of tail." The man turned around with a confused look on his face and said, "Make up your mind. Last night you told me to go fly a kite!"

AGREEMENT

A U.S. Marine fire team was marching north of Fallujah when they came upon an Iraqi terrorist, badly injured and unconscious. On the opposite side of the road was an American Marine in a similar, but less serious state. The Marine was conscious and alert and as first aid was given to both men, the squad leader asked the injured Marine what happened. The Marine reported, "I was heavily armed and moving north along the highway here and coming south was a heavily armed insurgent. We saw each other and both took cover in the ditches along the road.

I yelled to him that Saddam Hussein was a miserable low-life scum-bag who got what he deserved and he yelled back that Ted Kennedy is a fat, good-for-nothing, left wing liberal, drunk who doesn't know how to drive. So I said that Osama Bin Laden dresses and acts like a frigid, mean-spirited lesbian! He retaliated by yelling, Oh yeah? Well, so does Hillary Clinton!"

"And there we were in the middle of the road, shaking hands, when a truck hit us."

BUSINESS PROPOSAL

Justin wanted to have sex with a girl in his office, but she said she already had a boyfriend. One day he got so frustrated that he went up to her and said, "I'll give you a $100 if you let me have sex with you." The girl said, "NO!" Then Justin said, "I'll be fast. I'll throw the money on the floor, you bend down and I'll be finished by the time you pick it up." She thought for a moment and said she would have to consult her boyfriend. She called her boyfriend and told him the story. The boyfriend said, "Ask him for $200 and pick up the money real fast. He won't even be able to get his pants down." She agreed and accepted the proposal. A half an hour went by. Finally, after 45 minutes the boyfriend called and asked what happened. She said, **"The bastard used quarters!" Management lesson**: ALWAYS consider a business proposal in it's entirety before agreeing to it and getting screwed.

NOTICE

THIS DEPARTMENT REQUIRES NO PHYSICAL FITNESS PROGRAM.

EVERYONE GETS ENOUGH EXERCISE JUMPING TO CONCLUSIONS, FLYING OFF THE HANDLE, RUNNING DOWN THE BOSS, KNIFING FRIENDS IN THE BACK, DODGING RESPONSIBILITY, AND PUSHING THEIR LUCK.

ITALIAN BOY CONFESSES

"Bless me Father, for I have sinned. I have been with a loose woman." The priest asks, "Is that you, Alfred Angrisani?" "Yes, Father it is." "And who was the woman you were with?" "I can't tell you, Father. I don't want to ruin her reputation." "Well, Alfred, I'm sure to find out her name sooner or later, so you may as well tell me now. Was it Tina Minetti?" "I cannot say." "Was it Teresa Volpe?" "I'll never tell." "Was it Nina Capeli?" "I'm sorry, but I cannot name her." "Was it Cathy Piriano?" "My lips are sealed." "Was it Rosa Di Angelo, then?" "Please Father, I cannot tell you." The priest sighed in frustration. "You're very tight lipped, Alfred, and I admire that. But you've sinned and have to atone. You cannot attend church services for 4 months. Now you go and behave yourself." Alfred walks back to his pew where his friend Nino slides over and whispers, "What'd you get?" **"Four months vacation and five good leads."**

105

(Billie Jo, I made a note to find 'blank page cost'. ga).

"Yea, though I walk through the valley of the shadow of death, I will fear no evil" Psalm 23

CHAPTER 4

PHOTOS - HAVE AT LEAST ONE PAL!

MEN - MEN - MEN

Okay, it *FINALLY* all makes sense now...
I never looked at it this way before:
MENtal illness
MENstrual cramps
MENopause
GUYnecologist
And, when we have *REAL* trouble, it's a
HISterectomy
**Ever notice how the majority of women's problems start with
MEN?**

108

Sunday Morning Sex

I will never hear church bells ringing again without smiling... Upon hearing that her elderly grandfather had just passed away, Kelly went straight to her grandparent's house to visit her 95-year-old grandmother and comfort her.

When Kelly asked how her grandfather had died her grandmother replied, "He had a heart attack while we were making love on Sunday morning." Horrified, Kelly told her grandmother that 2 people nearly 100 years old having sex would surely be asking for trouble. "Oh no my dear," replied granny. "Many years ago, realizing our advanced age, we figured out the best time to do it was when the church bells would start to ring. It was just the right rhythm. Nice and slow and even. Nothing too strenuous, simply in on the Ding and out on the Dong."

She paused to wipe away a tear and continued, "He'd still be alive if the ice cream truck hadn't come along!"

Blonde - Cowboy

The Sheriff in a small town walks out in the street and sees, Dave, a blonde cowboy coming down the walk with nothing on but his cowboy hat, gun and boots. The Sheriff arrests him for indecent exposure. As he is locking him up he asks, "Why in the world are you walking around like this?"

Dave says, "Well it's like this Sheriff. I was in the bar down the road and this pretty little redhead asks me to go out to her motor home with her... so I did. We go inside and she pulls off her top and asks me to pull off my shirt... so I did. Then she pulls off her skirt and asks me to pull of my pants... so I did. Then she pulls off her panties and asks me to pull off my shorts... so I did. Then she gets on the bed and looks at me kind of sexy and says," "Now go to town cowboy!". . . And Dave said, "*So here I am!*"

JOB APPLICANTS - MATCH APPROPRIATE POSITION

You put 100 bricks in some particular order in a closed room with an open window. Then you send 2 or 3 candidates into the room and close the door. You leave them alone, come back after 6 hours and analyze the situation:

1. If they are counting the bricks, put them in the accounting department.
2. If they are recounting them, put them in auditing.
3. If they have messed up the whole place with the bricks, put them in engineering.
4. If they are arranging the bricks in some strange order, put them in planning.
5. If they are throwing the bricks at each other, put them in operations.
6. If they are sleeping, put them in security.
7. If they have broken the bricks into pieces, put them in information technology.
8. If they are sitting idle, put them in human resources.
9. If they say they have tried different combinations, yet not a brick has been moved, put them in sales.
10. If they have already left for the day, put them in marketing.
11. If they are staring out the window, put them in strategic planning.
12. If they are talking to each other and not a single brick has been moved, congratulate them and put them in top management.
13. Finally, if they have surrounded themselves with bricks in such a way that they can neither be seen nor heard from, put them in Congress.

PHOTOS - HOW TO HUG A BABY

Dui - TENNESSEE STYLE

Only a person in Tennessee could think of this!!! From the county where drunk driving is considered a sport, comes this absolutely true story. Recently a routine police patrol parked outside a bar in Paris, Tennessee. After last call the officer noticed a man (**DAVE**) leaving the bar so intoxicated that he could barely walk. Dave stumbled around the parking lot for a few minutes with the officer quietly observing. After what seemed an eternity the man managed to find his car and fall into it. He sat there for a few minutes as a number of other patrons left the bar and drove off.

Finally, Dave started the car and switched the wipers on and off. It was a nice, dry summer night. He flicked the blinkers on and off a couple of times, honked the horn and then switched on the lights. He moved the vehicle forward a few inches, reversed a little and remained still for a few more minutes as more patrons left. At last, when his was the only car left in the parking lot, he pulled out and drove slowly down the road. The police officer, having waited patiently all this time, started up his patrol car, put the flashing lights on and promptly pulled Dave over and administered a breathalyzer test. To his amazement the breathalyzer indicated no evidence that the man had consumed any alcohol at all! Dumbfounded, the officer said, "Dave, I'll have to ask you to accompany me to the police station. This breathalyzer equipment must be broken." "I doubt it," said Dave, a truly proud Hillbilly. **"Tonight I'm the designated decoy!"**

Photos - THE FOUR STAGES OF LIFE

111

AMAZINGLY SIMPLE HOME REMEDIES

1. If you are choking on an ice cube, don't panic. Simply pour a cup of boiling water down your throat and presto, the blockage will almost instantly be removed.

2. Clumsy? Avoid cutting yourself while slicing vegetables by getting someone else to hold them while you chop away.

3. You can avoid arguments with the Mrs. about lifting the toilet seat by just using the sink.

4. For people who suffer from high blood pressure, simply cut yourself and bleed for a few minutes, thus reducing the pressure in your veins. Remember to use an egg timer.

5. A mouse trap placed on top of your alarm clock will prevent you from rolling over and going back to sleep after you hit the snooze button.

6. If you have a bad cough, take a large dose of laxatives. Then you will be afraid to cough.

7. Have a bad toothache? Smash your thumb with a hammer and you will forget all about the toothache.

8. Sometimes, we just need to remember what the rules of life really are:
   In life, you only need two tools, WD-40 and duct tape
   If it doesn't move but should, use WD-40
   If it should not move and does, use the duct tape.

9. Remember: Everyone seems normal until you get to know them.

10. Never pass up an opportunity to go to the bathroom.

Thought for the day: Some people are like slinkies... They are not really good for anything... But they still bring a smile to your face when you push them down a flight of stairs.

MENOPAUSE JEWELRY

My husband, being unhappy with my mood swings, bought me a mood ring the other day so he would be able to monitor my moods. We've discovered that when I'm in a good mood it turns a beautiful blue-green. When I'm in a bad mood it leaves a big red mark on his forehead. Maybe next time he'll buy me a diamond.

PHOTOS - WHEN NOT TO TAKE A PHOTO

. . . the cow's out of the barn !

WIZZARD OF OZ AND 4 US PRESIDENTS

Four US Presidents get caught up in a tornado and are whirled away to the land of OZ. They finally made it to the Emerald City and went to find the Great Wizard. "What brings the 4 of you before me?" the Wizard asked. Jimmy Carter steps forward timidly and said, "I've come for some courage." "No problem." Richard Nixon steps forward, "Well, I think I need a heart." "Done!" Up steps Bush "I'm told by the American people I need a brain." "Consider it done." Then there is great silence in the hall. Clinton is just standing there looking around but says nothing. Irritated, the Wizard finally asks, "Well, what do you want?" . . . .

"IS DOROTHY HERE?"

CARTOONS
CHRISTMAS TREE

Is that a Christmas tree in your pocket, or are you glad to see me?

THE NUT CRACKER

THE DONKEY

One day a farmer's donkey fell down into a well. The animal cried pathetically for hours as the farmer tried to figure out what to do. Finally he decided the animal was old and the well needed to be covered up anyway. It just wasn't worth it to retrieve the donkey. He invited all his neighbors to come over and help him. They all grabbed a shovel and began to shovel dirt into the well. At first, the donkey realized what was happening and cried horribly. Then to everyone's amazement he quieted down. A few shovel loads later, the farmer finally looked down the well and was astonished at what he saw. With each shovel of dirt that hit his back, the donkey was doing something amazing. He would shake it off and take a step up. As the farmer's neighbors continued to shovel dirt on top of the animal, he would shake and take another step. Pretty soon everyone was amazed as the donkey stepped up over the edge of the well and happily trotted off.

Life is going to shovel dirt on you, all kinds. The trick to getting out is to shake it off and take another step. (The farmer died from an infected bite, which was received from the donkey!)

114

THE MAN WHO KNOWS HIS MATH

 I was driving to work yesterday when I observed a female driver who cut right in front of a pickup truck, causing the driver to drive into the shoulder to avoid hitting her. This evidently angered the driver enough that he hung his arm out his window and gave the woman the finger. "Man, that guy is stupid," I thought to myself.

I always smile nicely and wave in a sheepish manner whenever a female does anything to me in traffic and here's why: I drive 48 miles each way to work every day. That's 96 miles each day. Of these, 16 miles each way is bumper-to-bumper. Most of the bumper-to-bumper is on an 8 lane highway. There are 7 cars every 40 feet for 32 miles. That works out to 982 cars every mile or 31,424 cars. Even though the rest of the 32 miles are not bumper-to-bumper I figure I pass at least another 4000 cars. That brings the number to something like 36,000 cars that I pass every day. Statistically, females drive half of these.

That's 18,000 women drivers! In any given group of females 1 in 28 has PMS. That's 642. According to *Cosmopolitan*, 70% describe their love life as dissatisfying or unrewarding. That's 449. According to the *National Institute of Health*, 22% of all females have seriously considered suicide or homicide. That's 98. 34% describe men as their biggest problem. That's 33. According to the National Rifle Association, 5% of all females carry weapons and this number is increasing.

That means that EVERY SINGLE DAY I drive past at least one female that has a lousy love life, thinks men are her biggest problem, has seriously considered suicide or homicide, has PMS and is armed.......Give her the finger? *I don't think so!!!*

PHOTOS - WHY PETS BITE PEOPLE and HATE HALLOWEEN

115

TEENY-WEENIE MEDICAL PROBLEM

Darrell went to the doctor and said, "Doctor I've got a problem, but if you're going to treat it, first you've got to promise not to laugh." "Of course I won't laugh," the doctor said. "I'm a professional. In over twenty years I've never laughed at a patient." "Okay then," Darrell said and proceeded to drop his trousers, revealing the tiniest penis the doctor has ever seen. It couldn't have been the size of a peanut. Unable to control himself, the doctor started giggling then fell laughing to the floor. Ten minutes later he was able to struggle to his feet and regain his composure.

"I'm so sorry Darrell," said the doctor. "I really am...I don't know what came over me. On my honor as a doctor and a gentleman I promise it won't happen again...Now what seems to be the problem?" **"It's swollen."** Darrel replied.

CARTOONS - CONFIRMING GLOBAL WARMING

116

DICTIONARY

DICTIONARY FOR DECODING WOMEN'S PERSONAL ADS

1. 40-ish = 49
2. Adventurous = Slept with everyone
3. Athletic = No breasts
4. Average looking = Moooo
5. Beautiful = Pathological liar
6. Emotionally secure = On medication
7. Feminist = Fat
8. Free spirit = Junkie
9. Friendship first = Former slut
10. New-Age = Body hair in the wrong places
11. Old-fashioned = No BJs
12. Open-minded = Desperate
13. Outgoing = Loud and embarrassing
14. Professional = Bitch
15. Wants soul-mate = Stalker

DICTIONARY FOR DECODING WOMEN'S ENGLISH

1. Yes = No
2. No = Yes
3. Maybe = No
4. We need = I want
5. I'm sorry = You'll be sorry
6. We need to talk = You're in trouble
7. Sure, go ahead = You better not
8. Do what you want = You will pay for this later
9. I am not upset = Of course I'm upset, you moron!
10. You're certainly attentive = Is sex all you ever think about?

DICTIONARY FOR DECODING MEN'S ENGLISH

1. I'm hungry = I'm hungry
2. I'm sleepy = I'm sleepy
3. I'm tired = I'm tired
4. Nice dress = Nice cleavage!
5. I love you = Let's have sex now
6. I'm bored = Do you want to have sex?
7. May I have this dance? = I'd like to have sex with you
8. Can I call you sometime? = I'd like to have sex with you
9. Do you want to go to a movie? = I'd like to have sex with you
10. Can I take you out to dinner? = I'd like to have sex with you
11. I don't think those shoes go with that outfit = I'm gay

117

Barbie Variations

Barbie Variations

At long last, here are some NEW Barbie dolls to coincide with her and OUR aging gracefully. These are a bit more realistic:

1. Bifocals Barbie ~ Comes with her own set of blended-lens fashion frames in six wild colors (half frames too!), neck chain and large-print editions of *Vogue* and *Martha Stewart Living.*
2. Hot Flash Barbie ~ Press Barbie's bellybutton and watch her face turn beet red while tiny drops of perspiration appear on her forehead. Comes with handheld fan and tiny tissues.
3. Facial Hair Barbie ~ As Barbie's hormone levels shift, see her whiskers grow. Available with teensy tweezers and magnifying mirror.
4. Flabby Arms Barbie ~ Hide Barbie's droopy triceps with these new, roomier-sleeved gowns. Good news on the tummy front, two Moo-Moos with tummy-support panels are included.
5. Bunion Barbie ~ Years of disco dancing in stiletto heels have definitely taken their toll on Barbie's dainty arched feet. Soothe her sores with the pumice stone and then slip on her soft terry mules.

6. No-More-Wrinkles Barbie ~ Erase those pesky crow's-feet and lip lines with a tube of Skin Sparkle-Spackle from Barbie's own line of exclusive age-blasting cosmetics.
7. Soccer Mom Barbie ~ All that experience as a cheerleader is really paying off as Barbie dusts off her old high school megaphone to root for Babs and Ken, Jr.. Comes with minivan in robin-egg blue or white and a cooler filled with doughnut holes and fruit punch.
8. Mid-life Crisis Barbie ~ It's time to ditch Ken. Barbie needs a change and Alonzo, her personal trainer, is just what the doctor ordered along with Prozac. They're hopping into her new convertible and heading for the Napa Valley to open a B & B. Includes a real tape of 'Breaking Up Is Hard to Do'.
9. Divorced Barbie ~ Sells for $199.99. Comes with Ken's house, Ken's car and Ken's boat.
10. Recovery Barbie ~ Too many parties have finally caught up with the ultimate party girl. Now she does 'Twelve Steps' instead of dance steps. Clean and sober, she's going to meetings religiously. Comes with a little copy of 'The Big Book' and a six-pack of Diet Coke.
11. Post-Menopausal Barbie ~ This Barbie wets her pants when she sneezes, forgets where she puts things and cries a lot. She is sick and tired of Ken sitting on the couch watching the tube and clicking through the channels. Comes with Depends and Kleenex. As a bonus this year, the book 'Getting In Touch with Your Inner Self' is included.

BLACK LEATHER OUTFIT

When a woman wears leather clothing,
A man's heart beats quicker,
his throat gets dry,
he goes weak in the knees,
and he begins to think irrationally.

Ever wonder why?

BECAUSE SHE SMELLS LIKE A NEW TRUCK....

THE BOY AND THE LOVER

A woman takes a lover home during the day while her husband is at work. Her 9-year-old son comes home unexpectedly, sees them and hides in the bedroom closet to watch. The woman's husband also comes home unexpectedly. She puts her lover in the closet, not realizing that the little boy is already in there. The little boy says, "Dark in here." The man says, "Yes, it is."

Boy: "I have a baseball."
Man: "That's nice."
Boy: "Want to buy it?"
Man: "No thanks."
Boy: "My dad's outside."
Man: "OK, how much?"
Boy: "$250."

In the next few weeks, it happens again that the boy and the lover are in the closet together.
Boy: "Dark in here."
Man: "Yes, it is."
Boy: "I have a baseball glove."
The lover, remembering the last time, asks the boy, "How much?"
Boy: "$750."
Man: "Sold."

A few days later the father says to the boy, "Grab your glove, let's go outside and have a game of catch." The boy says, "I can't. I sold my baseball and my glove." The father asks, "How much did you sell them for?" The boy replies, "$1000." The father says, "That's terrible to overcharge your friends like that, that is way more than those two things cost. I'm going to take you to church and make you confess." They go to the church and the father makes the little boy sit in the confession booth and he closes the door. The boy says, "Dark in here."

The priest says, **"Don't start that crap** again; **you're in my closet now!"**

Photos - F*** PETE, IS THAT YOU?

Fuck! Pete, is that you???

Onions & CHRISTMAS TREES

A family is at the dinner table and the son asks his father, "Dad, how many kinds of boobies are there?" The father, surprised, answers, "Well son, there's three kinds of breasts. In   her twenties a woman's breasts are like melons, round and   firm. In her thirties and forties they're like pears, still nice   but hanging a bit.   After fifty, they are like onions." "Onions?" "Yes, you see them and they make you cry." This infuriated his wife and daughter so the daughter said, "Mum, how many kinds of 'willies' are there?" The mother, surprised, smiles and answers, "Well dear, a man goes through three phases, each like a different type of tree. In his twenties he is like an oak tree, mighty and hard.   In his thirties and forties he's like a birch tree, flexible but reliable. After his fifties, he's like a Christmas tree." "A Christmas tree?" "Yes, dead from the root up and the balls are just for decoration."

ADS FROM A LONG TIME AGO

Buy a dog

- If you want someone who will eat whatever you put in front of him and never says it's not quite as good as his mother made it... Then buy a dog.
- If you want someone always willing to go out at any hour, for as long and wherever you want... Then buy a dog.
- If you want someone who will never touch the remote, doesn't care about football and can sit next to you as you watch romantic movies... Then buy a dog.

- If you want someone who is content to get up on your bed just to warm your feet and whom you can push off if he snores... Then buy a dog.
- If you want someone who never criticizes what you do, doesn't care if you are pretty or ugly, fat or thin, young or old, who acts as if every word you say is especially worthy of listening to and loves you unconditionally, perpetually... Then buy a dog.
- BUT on the other hand, if you want someone who will never come when you call, totally ignore you when you come home, leave hair all over the place, walks all over you, run around all night and only come home to eat and sleep and acts as if your entire existence is solely to ensure his happiness... **THEN BUY A CAT!**

WHEN TO CALL IT A NIGHT

20 Clues Cindy and Loretta, notoriously ignore but, should realize when it's time to 'CALL IT A NIGHT'.

1. I have absolutely no idea where my purse is.
2. I believe that dancing with my arms overhead and wiggling my butt while yelling, "WOO-HOO!" is truly the sexiest dance move around.
3. I've suddenly decided I want to kick someone's ass and honestly believe I could do it, too.
4. In my last trip to 'pee' I realize I now look more like Tammy Faye Baker than the goddess I was just four hours ago.
5. I drop my 3:00 am Taco Bell burrito on the floor, which I'm eating even though I'm not the least bit hungry, pick   it   up and carry on eating it.
6. I start crying and telling everyone I see that I love them *soooo* much.
7. There are less than three hours before I'm due to start work.
8. I've found a deeper/spiritual side to the geek sitting next to me.
9. The man I'm flirting with used to be my 5th grade teacher.
10. The urge to take off articles of clothing, stand on the table and sing or dance becomes strangely overwhelming.
11. My eyes just don't seem to want to stay open on their own so I keep them half closed and think it looks exotically sexy.
12. I yell at the bartender who I think cheated me by giving me just lemonade, but that's just because I can no longer taste the vodka.
14. I think I'm in bed but my pillow feels strangely like the kitchen floor.
15. I start every conversation with a booming, "DON'T take this the WRONG WAY but..."
16. I fail to notice the toilet seat lid's down when I sit on it.
17. My hugs begin to resemble wrestling take-down moves.
18. I'm tired so I just sit on the floor wherever I happen to be standing (or falling off a barstool) and take a quick nap.
19. I begin leaving the buttons open on my button fly pants to cut down on the time I'm in the bathroom away from my drink.
20. I take my shoes off because I believe it's their fault that I'm having problems walking straight.

124

ASK AN AMERICAN INDIAN WHAT HAPPENS WHEN YOU DON'T CONTROL IMMIGRATION

HOMELAND SECURITY

Fighting Terrorism Since 1492

A GOOD THOUGHT - TRUE LOVE

A girl asked a guy if he thought she was pretty. He said, "No." She asked him if he would want to be with her forever and he said, "No." She then asked him if she were to leave would he cry and once again, he replied with a "No." She had heard enough. As she walked away, tears streaming down her face, the boy grabbed her arm and said, "You're not pretty, you're beautiful. I don't want to be with you forever. I NEED to be with you forever and I wouldn't cry if you walked away...I'd die."

Remember: A good friend will bail you out of jail but a true friend will be sitting right next to you saying, **"Damn! That was fun!"** "I can handle anything that life throws at me. I may not be able to handle it well or correctly or gracefully or with finesse or expediently, but I will handle it."

ATTORNEYS *(Dedicated to Doris)*

From a book called "Disorder in the American Courts"

Attorney: "Are you sexually active?"

Witness: "No, I just lie there."

Attorney: "What is your date of birth?"

Witness: "July 18th."

Attorney: "What year?"

Witness: "Every year."

Attorney: "What gear were you in at the moment of impact?"

Witness: "Gucci sweats and Reeboks."

Attorney: "This myasthenia gravis, does it affect your memory at all?"

Witness: "Yes."

Attorney: "And in what way does it affect your memory?"

Witness: "I forget."

Attorney: "You forget. Can you give us an example of something you forgot?"

Attorney: "How old is your son, the one living with you?"

Witness: "Thirty-eight or thirty-five, I can't remember which."

Attorney: "How long has he lived with you?"

Witness: "Forty-five years."

Attorney: "What was the first thing your husband said to you that morning?"

Witness: He said, "Where am I, Cathy?"

Attorney: "And why did that upset you?"

Witness: "My name is Susan."

Attorney: "Do you know if your daughter has ever been involved in voodoo?"

Witness: "We both do."

Attorney: "Voodoo?"

Witness: "We do."

Attorney: "You do?"

Witness: "Yes, voodoo."

Attorney: "Now doctor, isn't it true that when a person dies in his sleep, he doesn't know until the next morning?"

Witness: "Did you actually pass the bar exam?"

Attorney: "The youngest son, the twenty-year-old, how old is he?"

Witness: "Uh, he's twenty."

Attorney: "Were you present when your picture was taken?

"Witness: "Would you repeat the question?"

Attorney: "So the date of conception (of the baby) was August 8th?"
Witness: "Yes."
Attorney: "And what were you doing at that time?"
Witness: "Uh..."
Attorney: "She had three children, right?"
Witness: "Yes."
Attorney: "How many boys?"
Witness: "None."
Attorney: "Were there any girls?"
Attorney: "Can you describe the individual?"
Witness: "He was about medium height and had a beard."
Attorney: "Was this a male or a female?"
Attorney: "Is your appearance here this morning pursuant to a deposition notice which I sent to your attorney?"
Witness: "No, this is how I dress when I go to work."
Attorney: "Doctor, how many autopsies have you performed on dead people?"
Witness: "All my autopsies are performed on dead people."
Attorney: "Do you recall the time that you examined the body?"
Witness: "The autopsy started around 8:30 pm."
Attorney: "And Mr. Denton was dead at the time?"
Witness: "No, he was sitting on the table wondering why I was doing an autopsy on him!"
Attorney: "Are you qualified to give a urine sample?"
Witness: "Huh?"
Attorney: "Doctor, before you performed the autopsy, did you check for a pulse?"
Witness: "No."
Attorney: "Did you check for blood pressure?"
Witness: "No."
Attorney: "Did you check for breathing?"
Witness: "No."

Attorney: "So then it's possible that the patient was alive when you began the autopsy?"
Witness: "No."
Attorney: "How can you be so sure, Doctor?"
Witness: "Because his brain was sitting on my desk in a jar."
Attorney: "But could the patient have still been alive, nevertheless?"
Witness: "Yes, it is possible that he could have been alive and practicing law."

127

THE GUYS' RULES

Finally, the guys' side of the story. We always hear 'the rules' from the female side. Now here are the rules from the male side. These are OUR rules! Please note these are all numbered "1" ON PURPOSE!

1. Men are NOT mind readers.
1. Learn to work the toilet seat. You're a big girl. If it's up, put it down. We need it up, you need it down. You don't hear us complaining about you leaving it down.
1. Sunday sports. It's like the full moon or the changing of the tides. Let it be.
1. Shopping is NOT a sport. And no, we are never going to think of it that way.
1. Crying is blackmail.
1. *Ask* for what you want. Let us be clear on this one: Subtle hints do not work! Strong hints do not work! Obvious hints do not work! Just say it!
1. Yes and No are perfectly acceptable answers to almost every question.
1. Come to us with a problem only if you want help solving it. That's what we do. Sympathy is why you have girlfriends.
1. A headache that lasts for 17 months is a problem. See a doctor.
1. Anything we said 6 months ago is inadmissible in an argument. In fact, all comments become null and void after a couple of days.
1. If you won't dress like the Victoria's Secret girls, don't expect us to act like soap opera guys.
1. If something we said can be interpreted two ways and one of the ways makes you sad or angry, we meant the other one.
1. You can either *ask* us to do something OR *tell* us how you want it done. Not both. If you already know best how to do it, just do it yourself.
1. Whenever possible, please say whatever you have to say during commercials.
1. Christopher Columbus did NOT need directions and neither do we.

1. ALL men see in only 16 colors, like Windows default settings. Peach, for example, is a fruit, NOT a color. Pumpkin is also a fruit. We have no idea what mauve or taupe is.
1. If it itches, it will be scratched. We do that.
1. If we ask what's wrong and you say 'nothing', we will act like nothing's wrong. We know you are lying, but it's just not worth the hassle.
1. If you ask a question you don't want an answer to, expect an answer you don't want to hear.
1. When we have to go somewhere, absolutely anything you wear is fine...REALLY.
1. Don't ask us what we're thinking about unless you're prepared to discuss such topics as baseball, the shotgun formation, football or golf.
1. You have enough clothes.
1. You have too many shoes.
1. I am in shape. Round *IS* a shape!

Thank you for reading this. Yes, I know, I have to sleep on the couch tonight; but did you know men really don't mind that? It's like camping.

CARTOONS - NANEE NANEE

We do not stop playing because we grow old; we grow old because we stop playing.

WORK OR PLAY

A man wonders if having sex on the Sabbath is a sin because he is not sure if sex is work or play. So he goes to a priest and asks for his opinion. After consulting the Bible the priest says, "My son, after an exhaustive search, I am positive that sex is work and, therefore, not permitted on Sundays." The man thinks, "What does a priest know about sex?" So he goes to a Lutheran minister who, after all, is a married man and experienced in this matter. He queries the minister and receives the same reply, "Sex is work and therefore not for the Sabbath." Not pleased with the reply, he

 seeks out a Rabbi, a man of thousands of years' tradition and knowledge. The Rabbi ponders the question, then states, "My son, sex is definitely play." The man replies, "Rabbi, how can you be so sure when so many others tell me sex is work?" The Rabbi softly speaks, "My son, if sex were work, my wife would have the maid do it."

PHOTOS - WHERE DID THEY PUT THE REST OF HIM?

Where did they put the rest of him?

HISCOCK

130

Cake or Bed?

A husband is at home watching a football game when his wife interrupts and asks, "Honey, could you fix the light in the hallway? It's been flickering for weeks now."  He looks at her and says angrily, "Fix the light now? Does it look like I have a G.E. logo printed on my forehead? I don't think so!" The wife asks, "Well then, could you fix the refrigerator door? It won't close right." To which he replied, "Does it look like I have Westinghouse written on my forehead? I don't think so!" "Fine," she says, "then could you at least fix the steps to the front door? They're about to break." "I'm not a damn carpenter and I don't want to fix the steps," he says. "Does it look like I have ACE Hardware written on my forehead? I don't think so!" "I've had enough of you. I'm going to the bar!!!" So he goes to the bar and drinks for a couple of hours. He starts to feel guilty about how he treated his wife and decides to go home and help out.

As he walks into the house he notices the steps are already fixed. As he enters the house he sees the hall light is working. As he goes to get a beer he notices the refrigerator door is fixed. "Honey?" he asks, "how'd all this get fixed?" She said, "Well when you left, I sat outside and cried. A nice young man came along and asked me what was wrong and I told him. He offered to do all the repairs and all I had to do was either go to bed with him or bake him a cake." Her husband asked, "So what kind of cake did you bake him?" To which she replied, **"Helloooo...do you see Betty Crocker written on my forehead? I don't think so!!!"**

Remember - Dance

They say it takes a minute to find a special person, an hour to appreciate them, a day to love them, but an entire life to forget them. Take the time to live!!! Life is too short...

Dance Naked!!!

131

BLONDE - LUNCH GUY

An Irishman, a Mexican and a blonde guy were doing construction work on the scaffolding on the 20th floor of a building. They were eating lunch and the Irishman said, "Corned beef and cabbage! If I get corned beef and cabbage one more time for lunch, I'm going to jump off this building!" The Mexican opened his lunch box and exclaimed, "Burritos again! If I get burritos one more time, I'm going to jump off too!" The blonde guy opened his lunch and said, "Bologna again! If I get a bologna sandwich one more time, I'm jumping too!" The next day, the Irishman opened his lunch box, saw corned beef and cabbage and jumped to his death. The Mexican opened his lunch box, saw a burrito and jumped to his death. The blonde guy opened his lunch box, saw the bologna sandwich and jumped to his death as well.

At the funeral, the Irishman's wife was weeping. She said, "If I had known how tired he was of corned beef and cabbage, I never would have given it to him again!" The Mexican's wife also wept and said, "I could have given him tacos or enchiladas instead! I didn't realize he hated burritos so much." Everyone turned and stared at the Blonde's wife..."Hey don't look at me," she said, "he makes his own lunch!!!"

JOSE AND CARLOS

Jose and Carlos are panhandlers; they panhandle in different areas of town. Carlos panhandles just as long as Jose but only collects $8 or $9 dollars every day. Jose brings home a suitcase FULL of $10 dollar bills, drives a Mercedes, lives in a mortgage free house and has a lot of money to spend. Carlos says to Jose, "I work just as long and hard as you do but how do you bring home a suitcase full of $10 dollar bills every day?" Jose says, "Look at your sign, what does it say?" Carlos' sign reads, "I have no work, a wife and 6 kids to support." Jose says, "No wonder you only get $8 – 9 dollars." Carlos says, "What does your sign say?" Jose shows Carlos his sign; it reads, **"I only need another $10.00 to move back to Mexico."**

PHOTOS - WHY PETS BITE PEOPLE and HATE HALLOWEEN

HEBONICS (Thank you Mr. LaRusso)

The New York City school board has officially declared Jewish-English, now dubbed 'Hebonics', as a second language. Backers of the move say the city's school district is the first in the state to recognize Hebonics as a valid language and significant attribute of New York culture. According to Howard Schollman, linguistics professor at New York University and renowned Hebonics scholar, the sentence structure of Hebonics derives from middle and eastern European language patterns, as well as Yiddish. Prof. Schollman explains, "In Hebonics, the response to any question is usually another question plus a complaint that is implied or stated. Thus, "How are you?" may be answered, "How should I be, with my feet?" Schollman says that Hebonics is a superb linguistic vehicle for expressing sarcasm or skepticism. An example is the repetition of a word with 'sh' or 'shm' at the beginning. "Mountains, shmountains. Thay away. You want a nosebleed?" Another Hebonics pattern is moving the subject of a sentence to the end with it's pronoun at the beginning, "It's beautiful, that dress." Schollman says one also sees the Hebonics verb moved to the end of the sentence. Thus the response to a remark such as "He's slow as a turtle" could be "Turtle, Shmurtle! Like a fly in Vaseline he walks." Schollman provided the following examples from his textbook, Switched-On-Hebonics.

Question: "What time is it?"
English answer: "Sorry, I don't know."
Hebonic answer: "What am I, a clock?"

Remark: "I hope things turn out okay."
English Response: "Thanks."
Hebonic response: "I should BE so lucky!"

Remark: "Hurry up. Dinner's ready."
English response: "Be right there."
Hebonic response: "Alright already, I'm coming. What's the 'hurry' business? Is there a fire?"

Remark: "I like the tie you gave me; wear it all the time."
English response: "Glad you like it."
Hebonic response: "So what's the matter, you don't like the other ties I gave you?"

134

Remark: "Sarah and I are engaged."
English Response: "Congratulations!"
Hebonic response: "She could stand to gain a few pounds."

Question: "Would you like to go riding with us?"
English answer: "Just say when."
Hebonic remark: "Riding, shmiding! Do I look like a cowboy?"

To guest of honor at his/her birthday party:
English remark: "Happy birthday"
Hebonic response: "A year smarter you should become."

Remark: "A beautiful day."
English response: "Sure is."
Hebonic remark: "So the sun is out, what else is new?"

Answering a phone call from son:
English remark: "It's been a long time since you've called."
Hebonic remark: "You didn't wonder if I'm dead yet?"

JUST THREE THINGS

1. **Zero Gravity -** When NASA first started sending up astronauts, they quickly discovered that ball-point pens would not work in zero gravity. To combat this problem, NASA scientists spent a decade and $12 billion dollars developing a pen that writes in zero gravity, upside-down, on almost any surface including glass and at temperatures ranging from below freezing to over 300C. The Russians used a pencil...your taxes are due again...enjoy paying them

2. **Our Constitution -** They keep talking about drafting a Constitution for Iraq. Why don't we just give them ours? It was written by a lot of really smart guys and it's worked for over 200 years. Plus, we're not using it anymore.

3. **Ten Commandments -** The real reason that we can't have the Ten Commandments in a courthouse is that you cannot post "Thou Shalt Not Steal", "Thou Shalt Not Commit Adultery" and "Thou Shalt Not Lie" in a building full of lawyers, judges and politicians... It creates a hostile work environment.

135

MAXINE vs. MARTHA

Martha - Stuff a miniature marshmallow in the bottom of a sugar cone to prevent ice cream drips.

Maxine - Just suck the ice cream out of the bottom of the cone for Pete's sake! You are probably lying on the couch with your feet up eating it, anyway!

Martha -To keep potatoes from budding, place an apple in the bag with the potatoes.

Maxine – Buy Idaho-mashed potato mix and keep it in the pantry for up to a year.

Martha – When a cake recipe calls for flouring the baking pan, use a bit of the dry cake mix instead and there won't be any white mess on the outside of the cake.

Maxine – Go to the bakery! They'll even decorate it for you.

Martha – If you accidentally over-salt a dish while it's still cooking, drop in a peeled potato and it will absorb the excess salt for an instant 'fix-me-up'.

Maxine – If you over-salt a dish while you are cooking, that's too bad. Please recite with me the real woman's motto, "I made it, you will eat it and I don't care how bad it tastes!"

Martha – Wrap celery in aluminum foil when putting in the refrigerator and it will keep for weeks.

Maxine – Never heard of it!

Martha – Brush some beaten egg white over pie crust before baking to yield a beautiful glossy finish.

Maxine – Mrs. Smith's frozen pie directions do not include brushing egg whites over the crust, so I don't.

Martha – Cure for headaches: take a lime, cut it in half and rub it on your forehead. The throbbing will go away.

Maxine – Take a lime, mix it with tequila, chill and drink!

Martha – If you have a problem opening jars, try using latex dishwashing gloves. They give a non-slip grip that makes opening jars easy.

Maxine – Go ask that very cute neighbor if he can open it for you.

Martha – Don't throw out all that left-over wine. Freeze it into ice cubes for future use in casseroles and sauces.

Maxine – Left-over wine??? HELLO!!!

The trouble with bucket seats is that not everybody has the same size bucket.

Do you realize that in about 40 years, we'll have thousands of old ladies running around with tattoos?

Money can't buy happiness; but somehow it's more comfortable to cry in a Porsche than in a Hyundai.

Drinking makes some husbands see double and see single.

Living in a nudist colony takes all the fun out of Halloween.

After a certain age, if you don't wake up aching in every joint, you're probably dead.

DON'T ARGUE WITH A WELL-READ WOMAN

One morning, the husband returns after several hours of fishing and decides to take a nap. Although not familiar with the lake, the wife decides to take the boat out. She motors out a short distance, anchors and reads her book. Along comes the game warden in his boat. He pulls up alongside the woman and says, "Good morning, ma'am. What are you doing?" "Reading a book," she replies, (thinking, "isn't that obvious?"). "You're in a restricted fishing area," he informs her. "I'm sorry, officer, but I'm not fishing. I'm reading." "Yes, but you have all the equipment. For all I know you could start at any moment. I'll have to take you in and write you up." "If you do that, I'll have to charge you with sexual assault," says the woman. "But I haven't even touched you," says the game warden. "That's true, but you have all the equipment. For all I know you could start at any moment." "Have a nice day ma'am," and he left.

Moral: **Never argue with a woman who reads. It's likely she can also think.**

PARKING LOT DECOY - BANDIT (WARNING)!

I don't know how many of you shop at Sam's Club or Costco but this may be useful to know. I became a victim of a clever scam while out shopping. This happened to me and it could happen to you!

Here's how the scam works:
Two seriously good-looking 23 year old, well-built guys come over to your car as you are packing your shopping in the trunk. They're both shirtless and start wiping your windshield with a rag and Windex with their highly-defined chest muscles and rock-hard abs exposed. It's impossible not to look. When you thank them and offer them a tip they say, "No" and instead ask you for a ride to another Sam's Club or Costco. You agree and they get in the back seat. On the way, they start talking dirty about what they want to do to you. Then, one of them climbs over into the front seat and begins kissing you on your neck and begs you to pull over so he can make love to you! While this is going on, the other guy steals your purse! I had my purse stolen, twice on Thursday, yesterday and most likely tomorrow.

A LONG TRIP

A Northern California couple decided to go to Florida to thaw out during a particularly cold winter. They planned to stay at the same hotel where they spent their honeymoon 47 years earlier. Because of hectic schedules, it was difficult to coordinate their travel schedules. Al left California and flew to Florida on Thursday. Betty would fly down the following day. Al checked into the hotel and there was a computer in his room, so he decided to send an email to Betty. However, he accidentally left out one letter in her email address. Without realizing his error, Al sent the email. Meanwhile, somewhere in Houston, a widow had just returned home from her husband's funeral. He was a minister who was called home to glory following a heart attack. The widow decided to check her email expecting messages from relatives and friends. After reading the first message she screamed and fainted. The widow's son rushed into the room, found his mother on the floor and saw the computer screen which read:

To: My Loving Wife   **Subject:** I've Arrived   **Date:** 1-24-07
I know you're surprised to hear from me. They have computers here now and you are allowed to send emails to your loved ones. I've just arrived and have been checked in. I see that everything has been prepared for your arrival tomorrow. Looking forward to seeing you then! Hope your journey is as uneventful as mine was.
P.S. Sure is freaking hot down here!

PHOTOS - LIKE MOMMY

139

OFFICE REFERENCE RED BINDER

I have spent the last few days compiling a Master Reference Binder to help deal with internal office issues. Inside this binder you will find 'solutions' to everyday problems you may encounter. If you are having problems with the processes or you're having difficulty dealing with others wanting you to handle things differently; or if Friday won't come fast enough, come track down this red binder, which is usually found on or in my desk. It should help get you through your day.

PHOTOS - MEN ARE JUST BORN THIS WAY

REMOTE CONTROL - WOMAN'S

PHOTOS - MEN WHO WALK ON WATER

Three men in history have walked on water:
The 1st one was Christ - The 2nd one was the apostle Peter - **and then there was this guy, named JOSE...**

TEXAS DRINKING RULES

A Mexican drinks his beer and suddenly throws his glass in the air, pulls out his pistol and shoots the glass into pieces. He says, "In Mexico our glasses are so cheap, we don't need to drink from the same glass twice." An Iraqi, obviously impressed by this, drinks his beer, throws his glass into the air, pulls out his AK-47 and shoots the glass to pieces. He says, "In Iraq we have so much sand to make glasses that we don't need to drink out of the same glass twice either." The Texas boy, cool as a cucumber, picks up his beer, drinks it, throws his glass into the air, pulls out his gun, shoots the Mexican and the Iraqi and catches his glass. He says, "In America we have so many illegal aliens that we don't have to drink with the same ones twice."

REFLECTIONS - AS I MATURE

- I've learned that you cannot make someone love you. All you can do is stalk them, hope they panic and give in.
- I've learned that no matter how much you care, some people are just assholes.
- I've learned that it takes years to build up trust and it only takes suspicion, not proof, to destroy it.
- I've learned that you can get by on charm for about fifteen minutes. After that, you'd better have a big willy or huge boobs.
- I've learned that you shouldn't compare yourself to others; they're more screwed up than you think.
- I've learned that you can keep vomiting long after you think you're finished.
- I've learned that we are responsible for what we do, unless we're celebrities.
- I've learned that regardless of how hot and steamy a relationship is as first, the passion fades and there had better be a lot of money to take its place!
- I've learned that 99% of the time when something isn't working in your house, one of your kids did it.
- I've learned that people you care most about in life are taken from you too soon and all the less important ones just never go away.

CALMNESS IN OUR LIVES

By following simple advice as heard on the Dr. Phil show, you too can find inner peace. Dr. Phil proclaimed, "The way to achieve inner peace is to finish all the things you have started and have never finished." So I looked around my house to see all the things I started and hadn't finished. Before leaving the house for work this morning, I finished off a bottle of Merlot, a bottle of Zinfandel, a bottle of Bailey's Irish Cream, a bottle of Kahlua, a package of Oreos, the remainder of my old Prozac prescription, the rest of the cheesecake, some Doritos and a box of chocolates. You have no idea how flipping good I feel right now!!!

PHOTOS - ZOO FOR THE DAY WITH THE KIDS

How to tell if you live in Iowa

Here's what Jeff Foxworthy has to say about Iowa:

- If your local Dairy Queen is closed from September through May, you live in Iowa.
- If someone in a Home Depot offers you assistance and they don't work there, you live in Iowa.
- If you've worn shorts and a parka at the same time, you live in Iowa.
- If you've had a lengthy telephone call with someone who dialed a wrong number, you live in Iowa.
- If 'Vacation' means going anywhere south of Des Moines for the weekend, you live in Iowa.
- If you measure distance in square miles of farmland, you live in Iowa.
- If you know several people who have hit a cow more than once, you live in Iowa.
- If you have gone from 'heat' to 'A/C' in the same day and back again, you live in Iowa.
- If you can drive 75 mph through 2 feet of snow during a raging blizzard without flinching, you live in Iowa.
- If you install security lights on your house and garage, but leave both unlocked, you live in Iowa.
- If you carry jumper cables in your car and your wife knows how to use them, you live in Iowa.
- If the I-80 speed limit is 75 mph, you're going 90 and everyone is passing you, you live in Iowa.
- If driving is better in the winter because the potholes are filled with snow, you live in Iowa.
- If you know all 4 seasons: almost winter, winter, still winter and road construction, you live in Iowa.
- If you have more hours on your lawn mower and snow blower than miles on your car, you live in Iowa.
- If you find 10 degrees a 'little chilly', you live in Iowa.

OFFICE STREAKING RULES (Dedicated to Doris)

Streaking will be permitted as follows:

1. Females will streak on odd days. Males on even days.
2. Girls who have tattoos on the lower half of their bodies such as 'sock it to me' or 'what you see is what you get' will not be permitted to streak due to inspection regulations.
3. Men with tattoos such as 'let it all hang out' will not be permitted to streak. Also, men with tattoos of butterflies, roses or elves will streak with females.
4. Junior Executives may carry their brief cases while streaking; however, the usual rule applies, Junior Executives may never carry any business papers but may carry the usual, such as a box of Kleenex, lunch, wife's shopping list and Playboy magazine.
5. Girls with bust sizes larger than 36B must wear a bra while in the Drafting Room or around any Draftsman while inking. Girls smaller than 36B should not try to impress people by wearing a bra.
6. If you streak in any area where food is served, you must wear two hair nets. They will be available in the vending machine next to the coffee machine.
7. In the event your physical make-up is such that your sex cannot be determined, such as flat chests for girls or long hair on boys, you must wear a tag stating 'I'm a boy' or 'I'm a girl'. Tags will be attached on girls with hair pins or paper clips. On boys, with rubber bands. Please return paper clips and rubber bands to stationary closet after you finish streaking.
8. Girls may wear jewelry while streaking but in no event should they bend over to retrieve it if it should fall off, due to insurance regulations.
9. No female beyond her seventh month of pregnancy or those wishing to become pregnant may streak.
10. No mixed streaking in dark hallways, broom closets or under desks.

FORGOTTEN INFORMATION (Oliver North)

It was 1987. At a lecture, the other day, they were playing an old news video of Lt. Col. Oliver North testifying at the Iran-Contra hearings during the Reagan Administration. There was Ollie in front of God and his country getting the third degree, but what he said was stunning.

He was being drilled by a senator. "Did you not recently spend close to $60,000 for a home security system?" Ollie replied, "Yes, I did, sir." The senator continued, trying to get a laugh out of the audience, "Isn't that just a little excessive?" "No sir," continued Ollie. "No? And why not?" the senator asked. "Because the lives of my family and I were threatened." "Threatened? By whom?" the senator questioned. "By a terrorist, sir." Ollie answered. "Terrorist? What terrorist could possibly scare you that much?" "His name is Osama bin Laden, sir," Ollie replied. At this point the senator tried to repeat the name, but couldn't pronounce it, which most people back then probably couldn't. A couple of people laughed at the attempt. Then the senator continued, "Why are you so afraid of this man?" "Because, sir, he is the most evil person alive that I know of," Ollie answered. "And what do you recommend we do about him?" asked the senator. "Well, sir, if it were up to me, I would recommend that an assassin team be formed to eliminate him and his men from the face of the earth." The senator disagreed with this approach, and that was all that was shown of the clip.

By the way, the senator was Al Gore. Also, terrorist pilot Mohammad Atta blew up a bus in Israel in 1986. The Israelis captured, tried and imprisoned him. As part of the Oslo agreement, with the Palestinians, in 1993, Israel had to agree to release so-called 'political prisoners'. However, the Israelis would not release any with blood on their hands. The American President at the time, Bill Clinton, and his Secretary of State, Warren Christopher, *insisted* that all prisoners be released. Mohammad Atta was freed and eventually thanked the US by flying an airplane into Tower One of the World Trade Center on September 11, 2001.

This was reported by many of the American TV networks at the time the terrorists were first identified. It was censored in the US from all later reports.

ADS FROM A LONG TIME AGO

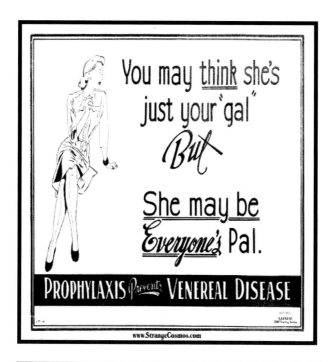

(Billie, the cost per blank page is $.014. ga)

150

CHAPTER 5

151

PHILOSOPHY BY CARLIN

1. Don't sweat the petty things and don't pet the sweaty things.
2. One tequila, two tequila, three tequila, floor.
3. Atheism is a non-prophet organization.
4. If man evolved from monkeys and apes, why do we still have monkeys and apes?
5. The main reason Santa is so jolly is because he knows where all the bad girls live.
6. I went to a bookstore and asked the saleswoman, "Where's the self-help section?" She said if she told me, it would defeat the purpose.
7. Could it be that all those trick-or-treaters wearing sheets aren't going as ghosts but as mattresses?
8. If a mute swears, does his mother wash his hands with soap?
9. If a man is standing in the middle of the forest and there is no one around to hear him, is he still wrong?
10. If someone with multiple personalities threatens to kill himself, is it considered a hostage situation?
11. Is there another word for synonym?
12. Isn't it a bit unnerving that doctors call what they do 'practice'?
13. Where do forest rangers go to 'get away from it all'?
14. What do you do when you see an endangered animal eating an endangered plant?
15. If a parsley farmer is sued, can they garnish his wages?
16. Would a fly without wings be called a walk?
17. Why do they lock gas station bathrooms? Are they afraid someone will clean them?
18. If a turtle doesn't have a shell, is it homeless or naked?
19. Why don't sheep shrink when it rains?
20. Can vegetarians eat animal crackers?
21. If the police arrest a mime, do they tell him he has the right to remain silent?

22. Why do they put Braille on the drive-through bank machines?
23. How do blind people know when they are done wiping?
24. How do they get the deer to cross at that yellow road sign?
25. Is it true that cannibals don't eat clowns because they taste funny?
26. What was the best thing before sliced bread?
27. One nice thing about egotists is that they don't talk about other people.

MORE CARLIN

1. Does the Little Mermaid wear an algae-bra?
2. Do infants enjoy infancy as much as adults enjoy adultery?
3. How is it possible to have a civil war?
4. If God dropped acid, would he see people?
5. If one synchronized swimmer drowns, do the rest drown too?
6. If you ate pasta and anti-pasta, would you still be hungry?
7. If you try to fail, and succeed, which have you done?
8. Whose cruel idea was it for the word 'Lisp' to have an 'S' in it?
9. Why are hemorrhoids called 'hemorrhoids' instead of 'asteroids'?
10. Why is it called tourist season if we can't shoot at them?
11. Why is the alphabet in that order? Is it because of that song?
12. Where are we going? And what's with this hand basket?
13. If the 'black box' flight recorder is never damaged during a plane crash, why isn't the whole damn airplane made out of that black stuff?
14. Why is there an expiration date on sour cream?
15. If you spin an oriental man in a circle three times, does he become disoriented?

BLONDE - FLORIDA or the MOON

Two blondes, living in California, were sitting on a bench talking. Tish says to the Janice, "Which do you think is farther away, Florida or the moon?" Janice replies, "Hellooooooooo, can you see Florida?"

EARLY RETIREMENT POLICY

To: All Employees **From:** Management **Location:** Division Office
As the result of the financial status of this corporation, immediate steps are being implemented to reduce the number of older employees and retain the younger, lower-paid employees throughout the company. This program to phase out older personnel through early retirement will be known as **RAPE** (Retire Aged People Early). Employees who are RAPED will be given the opportunity to look for other jobs outside the company. Also, if they are being RAPED, they can request review of their employment records before actual retirement. This phase of the program is called **SCREWED** (Survey of Capabilities of Retired Early Workers). All employees who have been RAPED and SCREWED may file an appeal with upper management. This will be called **SHAFT** (Study by the Higher Authority Following Termination). Under the terms of the new policy, employees may be RAPED once and SCREWED twice but may be SHAFTED as many times as the corporation deems appropriate.
If an employee follows the above procedures, he/she will be entitled to get **HERPES** (Half Earnings for Retired Personnel as Early Severance). Since HERPES is considered a benefit of the plan, any employee who has received HERPES will no longer be RAPED and SCREWED. The corporation wishes to assure the younger employees, who remain, that it will continue its policy to ensure that employees are well trained through **SHIT** (Special High Intensity Training) program. This company takes pride in the amount of SHIT our employees receive. We have given our employees more SHIT than other corporations in the world. However, if any employee feels that he/she does not receive enough SHIT on the job, see your immediate supervisor. Your supervisor is specially trained to make sure that you receive all the SHIT that you can stand.

AD - SINGLE BLACK FEMALE

SINGLE BLACK FEMALE seeks male companionship, ethnicity unimportant. I'm a very good girl who LOVES to play. I love long walks in the woods, riding in your pickup truck, hunting, camping and fishing trips. I love Cozy winter nights lying by the fire and candlelight dinners will have me eating out of your hand. I'll be at the front door when you get home from work wearing only what nature gave me. Call (555) 867-5309 and ask for Daisy. I'll be waiting....Over 15,000 men found themselves talking to the Atlanta Humane Society about an 8 week old black Labrador.

REDNECK VASECTOMY

A North Carolina couple, both bonafide rednecks, had 9 children. They went to the doctor to see about getting the husband 'fixed'. The doctor gladly started the required procedure and asked them what finally made them make the decision; why after nine children, would they choose to do this now? The husband replied that they had heard recently on the news that one out of every 10 children being born in the United States was Mexican and they didn't want to take a chance on having a Mexican baby because neither of them could speak Spanish.

155

THE GOOD WIFE'S GUIDE

- Have dinner ready. Plan ahead, even the night before to have a delicious meal ready on time for his return. This is a way of letting him know that you have been thinking about him and are concerned about his needs. Most men are hungry when they come home and the prospect of a good meal (especially his favorite dish) is a part of the warm welcome needed.

- Prepare yourself. Take 15 minutes to rest so you'll be refreshed when he arrives. Touch up your make-up, put a ribbon in your hair and be fresh looking. He has just been with a lot of work-weary people.

- Be a little gay and a little more interesting for him. His boring day may need a lift and one of your duties is to provide it.

- Clear away the clutter. Make one last trip through the main part of the house just before your husband arrives.

- Gather up schoolbooks, toys, paper etc. and then run a dishcloth over the tables.

- During the cooler months of the year, you should prepare and light a fire for him to unwind by. Your husband will feel he has reached a haven of rest and order. It will give you a lift, too. After all, catering for his comfort will provide you with immense personal satisfaction.

- Prepare the children. Take a few minutes to wash the children's hands and faces (if they are small), comb their hair and, if necessary, change their clothes. They are little treasures and he would like to see them playing the part. Minimize all noise. At the time of his arrival eliminate all noise of the washer, dryer or vacuum. Try to encourage the children to be quiet.

- Be happy to see him. (You're a good actress...)

- Greet him with a warm smile and show sincerity in your desire to please him.

- Listen to him. You may have a dozen important things to tell him but the moment of his arrival is not the time. Let

156

him talk first. Remember, his topics of conversation are more important than yours.

- Make the evening his. Never complain if he comes home late or goes out to dinner or other places of entertainment without you. Instead, try to understand his world of strain and pressure and his very real need to be home and relax.
- Your goal: Try to make sure your home is a place of peace, order and tranquility where your husband can renew himself in body and spirit.
- Don't greet him with complaints and problems.
- Don't complain if he's home late for dinner or even if he stays out all night. Count this as minor compared to what he might have gone through that day.
- Make him comfortable. Have him lean back in a comfortable chair or have him lie down in the bedroom. Have a cool or warm drink ready for him.
- Arrange his pillow and offer to take off his shoes. Speak in a low, soothing and pleasant voice.
- Don't ask him questions about his actions or question his judgment or integrity. Remember, he is the master of the house and as such will always exercise his will with fairness and truthfulness. You have no right to question him.
- A good wife always knows her place. . . .**I'm sorry, even my Grandmother wouldn't buy this crap!!!**

History Lesson

Abraham Lincoln was elected to Congress in 1846.
John F. Kennedy was elected to Congress in 1946.
Abraham Lincoln was elected President in 1860.
John F. Kennedy was elected President in 1960.
Both were particularly concerned with civil rights.
Both wives lost their children while living in the White House.
Both Presidents were shot on a Friday.
Both Presidents were shot in the head.
Now it gets really weird...
Lincoln's secretary was named Kennedy.
Kennedy's secretary was named Lincoln.
Both were assassinated by Southerners.
Both were succeeded by Southerners named Johnson.
Andrew Johnson, who succeeded Lincoln, was born in 1808.
Lyndon B. Johnson, who succeeded Kennedy, was born in 1908.
John Wilkes Booth, who assassinated Lincoln, was born in 1839.
Lee Harvey Oswald, who assassinated Kennedy, was born in 1939.
Both assassins were known by their three names.
Both names are composed of fifteen letters.
Lincoln was shot at a theater named 'Ford'.
Kennedy was shot in a car called 'Lincoln' made by 'Ford'.
Lincoln was shot in a theater and his assassin ran and hid in a warehouse.
Kennedy was shot from a warehouse and his assassin ran and hid in a theater.
Booth and Oswald were assassinated before their trials.
A week before Lincoln was shot, he was in Monroe, Maryland.
A week before Kennedy was shot, he was with Marilyn Monroe.

Photos - Pet positions

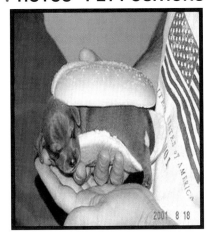 

 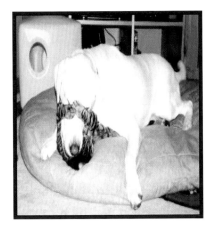

PERSONAL AD ON CRAIG'S LIST

What am I doing wrong?

Okay, I'm tired of beating around the bush. I'm a beautiful (spectacularly beautiful) 25-year-old girl. I'm articulate and classy. I'm not from New York. I'm looking to get married to a guy who makes at least half a million a year. I know how that sounds, but keep in mind that a million a year is middle class in New York, so I don't think I'm overreaching at all. Are there any guys who make $500K or more on this board? Any wives? Could you send me some tips? I dated a business man who makes around $200-250K but that's where I seem to hit a roadblock. $250,000 won't get me to Central Park West. I know a woman in my yoga class who is married to an investment banker and lives in Tribeca, and she's not as pretty as I am, nor is she a great genius. So what is she doing right? How do I get to her level?

Here are my questions specifically:

- Where do you single rich men hang out? Give me specifics i.e. bars, restaurants, gyms etc.
- What are you looking for in a mate? Be honest guys, you won't hurt my feelings.
- Is there an age range I should be targeting (I'm 25).
- Why are some of the women living lavish lifestyles on the Upper East Side so plain? I've seen really 'plain Jane' boring types who have nothing to offer, married to incredibly wealthy guys. I've seen drop dead gorgeous girls in singles bars in the east village. What's the story there?
- Jobs I should look out for? Everyone knows lawyer, investment banker, doctor. How much do they really make? And where do they hang out? And what about those hedge fund guys?

How do you decide marriage vs just a girlfriend? I am looking for MARRIAGE ONLY. Please hold your insults; I'm putting myself out there in an honest way. Most beautiful women are superficial; at least I'm being up front about it. I wouldn't be searching for this kind of guy if I weren't able to match him in looks, culture, sophistication and keeping a nice home and hearth.

160

Response:

I read your posting with great interest and have thought meaningfully about your dilemma. I offer the following analysis of your predicament. Firstly, I'm not wasting your time. I qualify as a guy who fits your bill; that is I make more than $500K per year. That being said, here's how I see it. Your offer, from the prospective of a guy like me, is plain and simple, a crappy business deal. Here's why: Cutting through all the BS, what you suggest is a simple trade, you bring your looks to the party and I bring my money. Fine, simple. But here's the rub, your looks will fade and my money will likely to continue into perpetuity...in fact, it is very likely that my income increases but it is an absolute certainty that you won't be getting any more beautiful! So, in economic terms you are a depreciating asset and I'm an earning asset. Not only are you a depreciating asset, your depreciation accelerates! Let me explain, you're 25 now and will likely stay pretty hot for the next five years, but less so each year. Then the fade begins in earnest. By 35, stick a fork in you! So in Wall Street terms, we would call you a trading position, not a buy and hold...hence the rub...marriage. It doesn't make good business sense to 'buy you' (which is what you're asking) so I'd rather lease. In case you think I'm being cruel, I would say the following: If my money were to go away, so would you, so when your beauty fades, I need an out. It's as simple as that. So a deal that makes sense is dating, not marriage.

Separately, I was taught early in my career about efficient markets. So I wonder how a girl as articulate, classy and spectacularly beautiful as you has been unable to find your sugar daddy. I find it hard to believe that if you are as gorgeous as you say you are that the $500K hasn't found you, if not only for a tryout. By the way, you could always find a way to make your own money and then we wouldn't need to have this difficult conversation. With all that said, I must say you're going about it the right way. Classic 'pump and dump'. I hope this is helpful and if you want to enter into some sort of lease, let me know.

161

PHOTOS - by 'GRAPHIC DAD'

PHOTOS - CHIPPENDALE REUNION THEN AND NOW

BEST LINE EVER

In summary, the police arrested Patrick Lawrence, a 22 year old, white male, in a pumpkin patch at 11:38pm on Friday night. On Monday, at the Gwinnet County, GA courthouse, Lawrence was charged with lewd and lascivious behavior, public indecency and public intoxication.

The suspect explained that as he was passing a pumpkin patch on his way home from a drinking session he decided to stop. "You know how a pumpkin is soft and squishy inside plus there was no one around for miles, at least I thought there wasn't anyone around," he stated in a telephone interview. Lawrence went on to say that he pulled over to the side of the road, picked out a pumpkin that he felt was appropriate for his purpose, cut a hole in it and proceeded to satisfy his alleged 'need'. "Guess I was really into it, you know?" he commented with evident embarrassment. In the process of doing the deed, Lawrence failed to notice an approaching police car and was unaware of his audience until Officer Brenda Taylor approached him.

"It was an unusual situation, that's for sure," said Officer Taylor. "I walked up to Lawrence and he's just banging away at this pumpkin." Officer Taylor went on to describe what happened when she approached Lawrence. I said, "Excuse me sir, but do you realize that you're having sex with a pumpkin?" He froze and was clearly very surprised that I was there and then he looked me straight in the face and said... "A pumpkin? Holy cow!!! **Is it midnight already?**"

163

DO YOU KNOW JACK SCHITT?

Jack Schitt is the only son of Aw Schitt, the fertilizer king, and Oh Schitt, the owner of the Knee Deep in Schitt Inn. Jack Schitt married Noe Schitt, and they had six kids. Their first little Schitt, Holy Schitt, passed on shortly after birth. Next came twin sons, Deep Schitt and Dip Schitt. They had two daughters, Fulla Schitt and Giva Schitt, and then another son, Bull Schitt. Deep Schitt married Dumb Schitt, a high school dropout. Dip Schitt married Alotta Schitt and they had one son, Chicken Schitt. Fulla Schitt and Giva Schitt married The Happens brothers. The Schitt-Happens children are Dawg Schitt, Byrd Schitt and Horse Schitt. Bull Schitt married an Italian girl, Pisa Schitt, and they had a baby named Hawg Schitt. They divorced and she remarried a man named Head. She now goes by the name Schitt-Head. If you have read this far and don't know who these people are, you probably didn't know Jack Schitt in the first place!

CARTOONS - SNOW BALL PET

I made myself a snowball,
As perfect as could be,
I thought I'd keep it as a pet,
And let it sleep with me.
I made it some pajamas,
And a pillow for its head,
Then last night it ran away,
But first-- it wet the bed.

PHOTOS - SISTERS' DAY

We are only as strong as the coffee we drink, the hairspray we use and the friends we have.

THE AMERICAN RESCUE MISSION

Rev. Elton Washington, Pastor, Dakota, Iowa:

Perhaps you have heard of me and my nationwide campaign for the cause of temperance. Each summer for the past fourteen years, I have toured the eastern United States and have delivered a series of lectures on the evils of drinking.

I have been accompanied each year by my young friend, Clyde Pasternak. Clyde, a young man of good family and excellent educational background, is a pathetic example of life ruined by excessive indulgence in whiskey and wild women. Clyde would appear with me at the lectures and sit on the platform staring at the audience through blood shot eyes, wheezing, sweating profusely, picking his nose, passing gas, fondling his genitals and making obscene gestures; where upon I would point him out as an example of what overindulgence can do to a person.

Unfortunately last fall, Clyde died. A mutual friend has given me your name and **I wonder if you would be available to take Clyde's place on my tour next year?**

With Reverential Awe,
Rev. Elton Washington, Pastor

165

HOROSCOPES – FUNNY

Aquarius (Jan 23 – Feb 18)

You have an inventive mind and are inclined to be progressive. You lie a great deal. On the other hand, you are inclined to be careless and impractical causing you to make the same mistakes over and over again. People think you are stupid.

Pisces (Feb 19 – Mar 20)

You have a vivid imagination and often think you are being followed by the CIA or FBI. You have minor influence over your associates and people resent you for flaunting your power. You lack confidence and are generally a coward. Pisces people do terrible things to small animals.

Aries (Mar 21 – Apr 19)

You are the pioneer type and hold most people in contempt. You are quick tempered, impatient and scornful of advice. You are not very nice.

Taurus (Apr 20 – May 20)

You are practical and persistent. You have a dogged determination and work like hell. Most people think you are stubborn and bull headed. You are a communist.

Gemini (May 21 – June 20)

You are a quick and intelligent thinker. People like you because you are bisexual. However, you are inclined to expect too much for too little. This means you are cheap. You are known for committing incest.

Cancer (Jun 21 – Jul 22)

You are sympathetic and understanding to other people's problems. They think you are a sucker. You are always putting things off. That's why you'll never make anything of yourself. Most welfare recipients are Cancer people.

Leo (Jul 23 – Aug 22)

You consider yourself a born leader. Others think you are pushy. Most Leo people are bullies. You are vain and dislike honest criticism. Your arrogance is disgusting. Leo people are known thieves.

Virgo (Aug 23 – Sept 22)

You are the logical type and you hate disorder. This nit-picking is sickening to your friends. You are cold and unemotional and sometimes fall asleep while making love. Virgos make good bus drivers.

Libra (Sept 23 – Oct 22)

You are the artistic type and have a difficult time with reality. If you are a man, you more than likely are a queer. Chances for employment and monetary gains are excellent. Most Libra women are good prostitutes. All Libras die of venereal disease.

Scorpio (Oct 23 – Nov 21)

You are shrewd in business and cannot be trusted. You shall achieve the pinnacle of success because of your total lack of ethics. Most Scorpio people are murdered.

Sagittarius (Nov 22 – Dec 21)

You are optimistic and enthusiastic. You have a reckless tendency to rely on luck since you lack talent. The majority of Sagittarians are drunks or dope fiends. People laugh at you a great deal.

Capricorn (Dec 22 – Jan 19)

You are conservative and afraid of taking risks. You don't do much of anything and are lazy. There has never been a Capricorn of any importance. Capricorns should avoid standing still too long as they tend to take root and become trees.

PHOTOS - TALK SHOW HOSTS (Italian vs. American)

What's wrong with this picture?

PHOTOS - REMEMBER in BLACK and WHITE

HALL OF FAME (Dedicated to Doris)

Dear Friend,

We have the distinguished honor of being on a committee for raising five million dollars for placing a statue of Richard M. Nixon in the Hall of Fame in Washington, D.C. This committee was in a quandary as to where to place the statue. It was thought not wise to place it beside the statue of George Washington, who never told a lie, nor beside Franklin D. Roosevelt, who never told the truth, since Richard Nixon could never tell the difference. We finally decided to place it beside Christopher Columbus, the greatest new dealer of them all. He left not knowing where he was going and upon arriving, did not know where he was. He returned not knowing where he had been and did it all on borrowed money.

Over 5000 years ago, Moses said to the children of Israel, "Pick up your shovels, mount your asses and camels and I will lead you to the Promise Land." Nearly 5000 years later, Roosevelt said, "Lay down your shovels, sit on your asses and light up a Camel, this *is* the Promise Land." Now, Nixon is stealing your shovels, kicking your asses, raising the price of camels and mortgaging the Promise Land. If you are one of the fortunate people who have any money left after paying taxes, we will expect a generous donation as contribution to this worthwhile project.   **Fraternally, Doris**

P.S. It is said that President Nixon is considering changing the Republican Party Emblem from an elephant to a condom because it stands for inflation, protects a bunch of pricks, halts production and gives a false sense of security while one is being screwed.

170

PHOTOS - WHEN IT IS OKAY TO SAY THE F*** WORD

PHOTOS - LAST ARGUMENT "We're here, Jeannie, its okay to come out now!"

MOM'S DRIVER'S LICENSE

A mother is driving a little girl to her friend's house for a play date. "Mommy," the little girl asks, "how old are you?" "Honey, you are not supposed to ask a lady her age," the mother replied. "It's not polite." "OK," the little girl says, "how much do you weigh?" "Now really," the mother says, "those are personal questions and are really none of your business." Undaunted, the little girl asks, "Why did you and Daddy get a divorce?" "That's enough questions, young lady, honestly!" The exasperated mother walks away as the two friends begin to play.

"My Mom won't tell me anything about her," the little girl says to her friend. "Well," says the friend, "all you need to do is look at her driver's license. It's like a report card, it has everything on it." Later that night the little girl says to her mother, "I know how old you are, you're 32." The mother is surprised and asks, "How did you find that out?" "I also know that you weigh 140 pounds." The mother is past surprised and shocked now. "How in heaven's name did you find that out?" "And," the little girl says triumphantly, "I know why you and daddy got a divorce." "Oh really?" the mother asks. "Why?"

"Because you got an 'F' in sex."

HEALTH PLANS

A wealthy hospital benefactor was being shown around the hospital by Dr. Lochner and Dr. Rodriquez. During her tour she passed a room where a male patient was masturbating furiously. "Oh my GOD!" screamed the woman, "That's disgraceful! Why is he doing that?" Dr. Lochner, who was leading the tour calmly explained, "I am very sorry that you were exposed to that but this man has a serious condition where his testicles rapidly fill with semen and if he doesn't do that at least 5 times a day, he'll be in extreme pain and his testicles could easily rupture.

"Oh, well in that case, I guess its ok," commented the woman. In the very next room, a male patient was lying in bed and it was obvious that a nurse was performing oral sex on him. Again, the woman screamed, "Oh my GOD! How can THAT be justified?" This time, Dr. Rodriquez spoke very calmly and said, **"Same illness, better health plan."**

PHOTOS - JAPANESE OCEAN DOME
Japanese Faux Inland Ocean/Beach w/Retractable Lid!!

Inside Dome with Lid Closed - (this is for real)!

EVERY WOMAN SHOULD KNOW

- A woman should have one old love she can imagine going back to and one who reminds her how far she has come.
- A woman should have enough money within her control to move out and rent a place of her own even if she never wants to or needs to.
- A woman should have something perfect to wear if her employer or date of her dreams wants to see her in an hour.
- A woman should have a youth she's content to leave behind.
- A woman should have a past juicy enough that she's looking forward to retelling it in her old age.

  - A woman should have a set of screw drivers, a cordless drill and a black lace bra.
  - A woman should have one friend who always makes her laugh and one who lets her cry.
  - A woman should have a good piece of furniture not previously owned by anyone else in her family.

- A woman should have eight matching plates, wine glasses with stems and a recipe for a meal that will make her guests feel honored.
- A woman should have a feeling of control over her destiny.
- Every woman should know how to fall in love without losing herself.
- Every woman should know how to quit a job, break up with a lover and confront a friend, without ruining the friendship and how to change a tire.
- Every woman should know when to try harder and when to walk away.
- Every woman should know that she can't change the length of her calves, the width of her hips or the nature of her parents.
- Every woman should know that her childhood may not have been perfect but its over.
- Every woman should know what she would and wouldn't do for love.
- Every woman should know how to live alone, even if she doesn't like it.
- Every woman should know whom she can and can't trust and why she shouldn't take it personally.
- Every woman should know when her soul needs soothing.
- Every woman should know what she can and can't accomplish in a day, a month and in a year.

REFLECTIONS - BEAUTIFUL WOMEN (Audrey Hepburn)

For attractive lips, speak words of kindness. For lovely eyes, seek out the good in people. For a slim figure, share your food with the hungry. For beautiful hair, let a child run his/her fingers through it once a day. For poise, walk with the knowledge that you never walk alone. People, even more than things, have to be restored, renewed, revived, reclaimed and redeemed. Never throw out anyone. Remember, if you ever need a helping hand, you will find one at the end of each of your arms. As you grow older, you will discover that you have two hands, one for helping yourself and the other for helping others.

THE ACCIDENT

A woman and a man are involved in a car accident on a snowy, cold Monday morning; it's a bad one. Both of their cars are totally demolished but, amazingly, neither of them is hurt. God works in mysterious ways. After they crawl out of their cars, the woman says, "So, you're a man. That's interesting. I'm a woman. Wow, just look at our cars! There's nothing left, but we're unhurt. This must be a sign from God that we should meet and be friends and live together in peace for the rest of our days." Flattered, the man replies, "Oh yes, I agree with you completely, this must be a sign from God!" The woman continues, "And look at this, here's another miracle. My car is completely demolished but this bottle of wine didn't break. Surely God wants us to drink this wine and celebrate our good fortune." Then she hands the bottle to the man. The man nods his head in agreement, opens it, drinks half the bottle and hands it back to the woman. The woman takes the bottle and immediately puts the cap back on and hands it back to the man. The man asks, "Aren't you having any?" The woman replies, "No. I think I'll just wait for the police."

Moral of the story: Women are evil. Don't mess with them.

175

SIGNS - SIGN OF WHAT?

PROVERBS #1 (Thank you Mr. LaRusso)

- A man is not honest simply because he never had a chance to steal.
- Don't judge a man by the words of his mother; listen to the comments of his neighbors.
- If the rich could hire other people to die for them, the poor could make a wonderful living.
- The wise man, even when he holds his tongue, says more than the fool when he speaks.
- Ask about your neighbors and then buy the house.
- What you don't see with your eyes, don't invent with your mouth.
- A hero is someone who can keep his mouth shut when he is right.
- One old friend is better than two new ones.
- When a thief kisses you, count your teeth.
- One of life's greatest mysteries is how the boy, who wasn't good enough to marry your daughter, can be the father of the smartest grandchild in the world.

PHOTOS - '911' THE USS NEW YORK

Built with 24 tons of scrap steel from the World Trade Center.

SIGNS - FAMILY PLANNING

PHOTOS - PROTESTORS (PRICELESS)

Protestors asked an American to translate their
protest slogans into English !!!

BEST RUM CAKE EVER (Dedicated to Doris)

1 cup butter

2 qts rum

1 tsp sugar

2 large eggs

1 cup dried fruit, baking powder, lemon juice and nuts

Sample the rum to ensure its quality and check its temperature. Select a large mixing bowl. Heat oven to 350. Confirm the rum's temperature by filling a measuring cup & drinking in one swallow. With electric mixer, beat one cup of butter in a large fluffy bowl. Add one seaspoon of thugar and beat again. Check again on rum flavor, opening 2nd quart if necessary. Add 2 arge leggs, 2 cups fried druit and beat rill high. If the druit gets stuck in beaters, pry loose with drewscriver. Sample rum again, checking for tonscisciticity. Next, sift 3 cups of salt or pepper. Sift in half pint of lemon juice. Fold in chopped butter with strained nuts. Add 1 babblespoon of brown thugar. Wix mel. Grease oven and turn cake pan 350 degrees. Pour whole mess in coven and ake. Test rum once again and go to bed.

PAPER JAM

A co-worker got a pen stuck inside our printer while trying to remove a jammed piece of paper. He started to try to remove the pen, but I told him we didn't have time for that now and to just put a note on the printer telling folks not to use it and then report it to the Help Desk. So he grabbed a piece of paper and scrawled on it. I left before he finished the note. About 20 minutes later one of my techs comes in laughing and said he was just in the lobby, saw a piece of paper on the printer and went to investigate. Attached is what he found.

Cartoons - A FRIEND IS LIKE A GOOD BRA #2

A friend is like a good bra: Hard to find, supportive, comfortable, always lifts you up, never lets you down or leaves you hanging and is always close to your heart.

Life CYCLE - REVERSAL

I think the life cycle is all backwards. You should start out dead; get it out of the way. You wake up in an old folk's home feeling better every day. You get kicked out for being too healthy, go collect your pension, then when you start work, you get a gold watch on your first day. You work 40 years until you're young enough to enjoy your retirement. You drink alcohol, you party, you're generally promiscuous and you get ready for High School. You go to primary school, you become a kid, you play, you have no responsibilities, you become a baby and then you spend your last 9 months floating peacefully with luxuries like central heating and room service on tap every day and then you finish off as an orgasm!!! It's got to be better this way because getting old sucks! **Lovingly, Uncle Howard**

Who HAS BETTER FRIENDS

Friendship Between Women: A woman didn't come home one night. The next day she told her husband that she had slept over at a friend's house. The man called his wife's 10 best friends. None of them knew about it.

Friendship Between Men: A man didn't come home one night. The next day he told his wife he had slept over at a friend's house. The woman called her husband's 10 best friends. Eight of them confirmed that he had slept over and two claimed that he was still there.

PHOTOS - USES OF STICKY NOTES

CREATION

A man said to his wife one day, "I don't know how you can be so stupid and so beautiful all at the same time." The wife responded, "Allow me to explain. God made me beautiful so you would be attracted to me. God made me stupid so I would be attracted to *you!*"

FOUR CORPORATE LESSONS (I Think Bill Mouren Wrote This One)!

Lesson #1

A man is getting into the shower, just as his wife is finishing up her shower, when the doorbell rings. The wife quickly wraps herself in a towel and runs downstairs. When she opens the door, there stands Bob, the next door neighbor. Before she says a word, Bob says, "I'll give you $800 to drop that towel." After thinking for a moment, the woman drops her towel and stands naked in front of Bob. After a few seconds, Bob hands her $800 dollars and leaves. The woman wraps back up in the towel and goes back upstairs. When she gets to the bathroom her husband asks, "Who was that?"

"It was Bob, the next door neighbor," she replies. "Great!" the husband says. "Did he say anything about the $800 he owes me?"

Moral of the story: If you share critical information pertaining to credit and risk with your shareholders, in time, you may be in a position to prevent avoidable exposure.

Lesson #2

A sales rep, an administration clerk and the manager are walking to lunch when they find an antique oil lamp. They rub it and a Genie comes out. The Genie says, "I'll give each of you just one wish." "Me first! Me first!" says the admin. clerk. "I want to be in the Bahamas, driving a speedboat without a care in the world." Poof! She's gone. "Me next! Me next!" says the sales rep. "I want to be in Hawaii, relaxing on the beach with my personal masseuse, an endless supply of Pina Coladas and the love of my life." Poof! He's gone. "OK, you're up," the Genie says to the manager. The manager says, "I want those two back in the office after lunch."

Moral of the story: Always let your boss have the first say.

Lesson #3

A crow was sitting on a tree doing nothing all day. A rabbit asked him, "Can I also sit like you and do nothing all day long?" The crow answered, "Sure, why not." So the rabbit sat on the ground below the crow and rested. A fox jumped on the rabbit and ate it.

Moral of the story: To be sitting and doing nothing, you must be sitting very high up.

Lesson #4

A turkey was chatting with a bull. "I would love to be able to get to the top of that tree," sighed the turkey, "but I haven't got the energy." "Well, why don't you nibble on my droppings?" replied the bull. "They're packed with nutrients." The turkey pecked at a lump of dung and found that it gave him enough strength to reach the lowest branch of the tree. The next day, after eating some more dung, he reached the second branch. Finally, after a forth night, there he was, proudly perched at the top of the tree. Soon he was spotted by a farmer who shot the turkey out of the tree.

Moral of the story: Bullshit might get you to the top, but it won't keep you there.

MID-LIFE CRISIS - MALE

When I was married, 25 years ago, I took a look at my wife one day and said, "Honey, 25 years ago we had a cheap apartment, a cheap car, slept on a sofa bed, watched a 10" black and white TV and I got to sleep every night with a 25-year-old brunette. Now we have a $500K home, a $45k car, a nice big bed, a plasma screen TV and I am sleeping with a 50-year-old woman.

My wife is a very reasonable woman. She told me to go out and find a hot 25 year old brunette, blonde or redhead and she would make sure that I would once again be living in a cheap apartment, driving a cheap car, sleeping on a sofa bed and watching a 10" black and white TV.

Aren't older women great? They really know how to solve your mid-life crisis!

IRS PENCIL SHARPENER

PHOTOS - REMEMBER in COLOR

PHOTOS - RARE PINK DOLPHIN

REFLECTIONS - IF I HAD MY LIFE TO LIVE OVER
(Erma Bombeck)

I would have gone to bed when I was sick instead of pretending the earth would go into a holding pattern if I weren't there for the day. I would have burned the pink candle sculpted like a rose before it melted in storage. I would have talked less and listened more. I would have invited friends over to dinner even if the carpet was stained or the sofa faded. I would have eaten the popcorn in the 'good' living room and worried much less about the dirt when someone wanted to light a fire in the fireplace. I would have taken the time to listen to my grandfather ramble about his youth. I would have shared more of the responsibility carried by my husband. I would never have insisted the car windows be rolled up on a summer day because my hair had just been teased and sprayed. I would have sat on the lawn with my grass stains. I would have cried and laughed less while watching television and more while watching life. I would never have bought anything just because it was practical, wouldn't show soil or was guaranteed to last a lifetime. Instead of wishing away nine months of pregnancy, I'd have cherished every moment and realized that the wonderment growing inside me was the only chance in life to assist God in a miracle. When my kids kissed me impetuously, I would never have said, "Later. Now go get washed up for dinner." There would have been more 'I love you's'. More 'I'm sorry's'. But mostly, given another shot at life, I would seize every minute, look at it and really see it, live it and never give it back. Stop sweating the small stuff. Don't worry about who doesn't like you, who has more or who's doing what. Instead, let's cherish the relationships we have with those who do love us. Let's think about what God HAS blessed us with and what we are doing each day to promote ourselves mentally, physically and emotionally.

- Age 3: She looks at herself and sees a Queen.
- Age 8: She looks at herself and sees Cinderella.
- Age 15: She looks at herself and sees an Ugly Sister (Mum, I can't go to school looking like this!).
- Age 20: She looks at herself and sees 'too fat/too thin, too short/too tall, too straight/too curly', but decides she's going out anyway.
- Age 30: She looks at herself and sees 'too fat/too thin, too short/too tall, too straight/too curly', but decides she doesn't have time to fix it, so she's going out anyway.
- Age 40: She looks at herself and sees 'clean' and goes wherever she wants to go.
- Age 50: She looks at herself and sees 'I am' and goes wherever she wants to go.
- Age 60: She looks at herself and reminds herself of all the people who can't even see themselves in the mirror anymore. She goes out and conquers the world.
- Age 70: She looks at herself and sees wisdom, laughter and ability. She goes out and enjoys life.
- Age 80: She doesn't bother to look. Just puts on a purple hat and goes out and enjoys life.

PHOTOS - VIRGINS IN HEAVEN

Much to their surprise, the Virgins awaiting Muslims in Heaven were not quite what they expected..

185

PHOTOS - PET POSITIONS

THE LONELY WIDOW

A lonely 70 year old widow, decided that it was time to get married again. She put an ad in the local newspaper that read:

Husband Wanted: must be in my age group, 70's, must not beat me, must not run around on me and must still be good in bed! All applicants please apply in person.

On the second day, she heard the doorbell. Much to her dismay, she opened the door to see a gray-haired gentleman sitting in a wheelchair. He had no arms or legs. "You're not really asking me to consider you, are you?" the widow asked. "Just look at you, you have no legs!" The old gentleman smiled, "Therefore, I cannot run around on you." "You have no arms either!" she snorted. Again, the old man smiled, "Therefore, I can never beat you." She raised an eyebrow and asked intently, "Are you still good in bed?" The old man leaned back, beamed a big smile and said, "I rang the doorbell didn't I?" The wedding is scheduled for Saturday.

PHOTOS - ROMANTIC GENTLEMEN (universal trait!)

187

THINGS TO SAY WHEN DRUNK

THINGS THAT JOANN FINDS **DIFFICULT** TO SAY WHEN DRUNK

- Innovative
- Preliminary
- Proliferation
- Cinnamon

THINGS THAT SUSIE FINDS **VERY DIFFICULT** TO SAY WHEN DRUNK

- Specificity
- British Constitution
- Passive aggressive disorder
- Transubstantiate

THINGS THAT PAM FINDS **DOWNRIGHT IMPOSSIBLE** TO SAY WHEN DRUNK

- Thanks, but I don't want to sleep with you
- Nope, no more booze for me!
- Sorry, but you are not really my type.
- Taco Bell? No thanks, I'm not hungry.
- Good evening, officer. Isn't it lovely out tonight?
- Oh, I couldn't! No one wants to hear me sing.
- I'm not interested in fighting you.
- Thank you, but I won't make any attempt to dance, I have no coordination. I'd hate to look like a fool.
- Where is the nearest bathroom? I refuse to pee in this parking lot or on the side of the road.
- I must be going home now, as I have to work in the morning.

SIGNS - SIGN OF WHAT?

EVE and ADAM

"Lord, I have a problem." "What's the problem, Eve?" "I know that you created me and provided this beautiful garden with all of these wonderful animals, as well as that hilarious comedic snake, but I'm just not happy." "And why is that Eve?" "Lord, I'm lonely and I'm sick to death of apples." "Well, Eve, in that case, I have a solution. I shall create a man for you."

"Man? What is that, Lord?" "A flawed creature with many bad habits and traits. He'll lie, cheat and be vain. All in all, he'll give you a hard time. But he'll be bigger and faster and will like to hunt and kill things. I'll create him in such a way that he will satisfy your physical needs. He will be witless and will revel in childish things like fighting and kicking a ball about."

"He won't be as smart as you, so he will also need your advice to think properly." "Sounds great," says Eve, with ironically raised eyebrows. "But what's the catch, Lord?"

"Well ... You can have him on one condition." "And what's that Lord?" "As I said, he'll be proud, arrogant and self-admiring ... So you'll have to let him believe that I made him first. And it will have to be our little secret ... **you know, woman to woman."**

PHOTOS - PRETTIEST KITTY EVER!

(Gwen, I'm getting tired. Billie Jo, quit whining!)

CHAPTER 6

THE PARROT (for Keith)

A woman went to a pet shop and immediately spotted a large, beautiful parrot. There was a sign on the cage that said $50.00. "Why so little?" she asked the pet store owner. The owner looked at her and said, "Look, I should tell you first that this bird used to live in a house of prostitution and sometimes says some pretty vulgar stuff."

The woman thought about this, but decided she had to have the bird anyway. She took it home and hung the bird's cage up in her living room and waited for it to say something. The bird looked around the room, then at her, and said, "New house, new madam." The woman was a bit shocked at the implication but then thought, "That's really not so bad."

When her 2 teenage daughters returned from school the bird saw them and said, "New house, new madam, new girls." The girls and the woman were a bit offended but then began to laugh about the situation considering how and where the parrot had been raised. Moments later the woman's husband, Keith, came home from work. The bird looked at him and said, **"Hi, Keith!"**

BLONDE - SUN

A Russian, an American and a Swedish Blonde were talking one day. The Russian said, "We were the first in space!" The American said, "We were the first on the moon!" The Blonde, Kirsten, said, "So what? We're going to be the first on the sun!" The Russian and the American looked at each other and shook their heads. "You can't land on the sun, you idiot! You'll burn up!" said the Russian. Kirsten replied, "We're not stupid, you know. We're going at night!"

Photos - remember in color

LEARN CHINESE IN 5 MINUTES - (read out loud)

ENGLISH	CHINESE
That's not right	Sum Ting Wong
Are you harboring a fugitive?	Hu Yu Hai Ding
See me ASAP	Kum Hia Nao
Stupid Man	Dum Fuk
Small Horse	Tai Ni Po Ni
Did you go to the beach?	Wai Yu so Tan
I bumped into a coffee table	Ai Bang Mai Fu Kin Ni
I think you need a face lift	Chin Tu Fat
I thought you were on a diet	Wai Yu Mun Ching
This is a tow away zone	No Pah King
Our meeting is scheduled for next week	Wai Yu Kum Nao
Staying out of sight	Lei Ying Lo
He's cleaning his automobile	Wa Shing Ka
Your body odor is offensive	Yu Stin Ki Pu
Great	Fa Kin Su Pa

PHOTOS - COMPUTER AIRBAGS

194

OPINION OF SEX BY VARIOUS CELEBRITIES

- "I believe that sex is one of the most beautiful, natural, wholesome things that money can buy."
- "You know 'that look' women get when they want sex? Me neither."
- "Having sex is like playing bridge. If you don't have a good partner, you'd better have a good hand."
- "Bisexuality immediately doubles your chances of a date on Saturday night."
- "There are a number of mechanical devices which increase sexual arousal, particularly in women. Chief among these is the Mercedes-Benz 380SL."
- "Leaving sex to the feminists is like letting your dog vacation at the taxidermist."
- "Sex, at age 90, is like trying to shoot pool with a rope."
- "Women might be able to fake orgasms, but men can fake whole relationships."
- "My girlfriend always laughs during sex; no matter what she's reading."
- "My mother never saw the irony in calling me a son-of-a-bitch."
- "A man might forget where he parks or where he lives, but he never forgets oral sex no matter how bad it is."
- "Ah, yes, divorce, from the Latin word meaning to rip out a man's genitals through his wallet."
- "Women complain about premenstrual syndrome, but I think of it as the only time of the month that I can be myself."
- "Women need a reason to have sex. Men just need a place."
- "According to a new survey, women say they feel more comfortable undressing in front of men than they do undressing in front of other women. They say that women are too judgmental, where, of course, men are just grateful."
- "There's a new medical crisis. Doctors are reporting that many men are having allergic reactions to latex condoms. They say they cause severe swelling. So, what's the problem?"
- "There's very little advice in men's magazines, because men think, 'I know what I'm doing', just show me somebody naked."
- "Instead of getting married again, I'm going to find a woman I don't like and just give her a house."
- "See, the problem is that God gives men a brain and a penis and only enough blood to run one at a time."

195

BIRTHDAY PRESENT

Dear Diary,

For my sixtieth birthday this year, my daughter (the dear) purchased a week of personal training at the local health club for me. Although I am still in great shape, since being a high school cheerleader 43 years ago, I decided it would be a good idea to go ahead and give it a try. I called the club and made my reservations with a personal trainer, named Erika, who identified herself as a 26 year old aerobics instructor and model for athletic clothing and swim wear. My daughter seemed pleased with my enthusiasm to get started. The club encouraged me to keep a diary to chart my progress.

Monday: Started my day at 6:00 am. Though to get out of bed, but found it was well worth it when I arrived at the health club to find Erika waiting for me. She is something of a Greek goddess, with blonde hair, dancing eyes and a dazzling white smile. Woo-Hoo! Erika gave me a tour and showed me the machines. I enjoyed watching the skillful way in which she conducted her aerobics class after my workout today. Very inspiring! Erika was encouraging as I did my sit-ups, although my gut was already aching from holding it in the whole time she was around. This is going to be a FANTASTIC week!!

Tuesday: I drank a whole pot of coffee, but I finally made it out the door. Erika made me lie on my back and push a heavy iron bar into the air; then she put weights on it! My legs were a little wobbly on the treadmill, but I made the full mile. Erika's rewarding smile made it all worthwhile. I feel GREAT! It's a whole new life for me.

Wednesday: The only way I can brush my teeth is by laying the toothbrush on the counter and moving my mouth back and forth over it. I believe I have a hernia in both pectorals. Driving was OK, as long as I didn't try to steer or stop. I parked on top of a GEO in the club parking lot. Erika was impatient with me, insisting that my screams bothered other club members. Her voice is a little too perky for that early in the morning, and when she scolds, she gets this nasally whine that is VERY annoying. My chest hurt when I got on the treadmill, so Erika put me on the stair 'monster'. Why the h*** would anyone invent a machine to simulate an activity rendered obsolete by elevators? Erika told me it would help me get in shape and enjoy life. She said some other s*** too.

Thursday: Erika was waiting for me with her vampire-like teeth exposed, as her thin, cruel lips were pulled back in a full snarl. I couldn't help being half an hour late; it took me that long to tie my shoes. Erika took me to work out with dumbbells. When she wasn't looking I ran and hid in the restroom. She sent another skinny b**** to find me. Then, as punishment, she put me on the rowing machine, which I sank!

Friday: I hate that b**** Erika more than any other human being has ever hated another human being in the history of the world. Stupid, skinny, anemic, anorexic little cheerleader. If there was a part of my body I could move, without unbearable pain, I would beat her with it. Erika wanted me to work on my triceps. I don't have any triceps! And, if you don't want dents in the floor, don't hand me the d*** barbells or anything that weighs more than a sandwich. Why couldn't it have been someone softer, like the drama coach or the choir director?

Saturday: Erika left a message on my answering machine in her grating, shrilly voice wondering why I did not show up today. Just hearing her made me want to smash the machine with my planner. However, I lacked the strength to even use the TV remote and ended up catching eleven straight hours of the Weather Channel.

Sunday: I had the Church van pick me up for services today so I could go and thank God that the week is over. I will also pray that next year my daughter (the little s***) will choose a gift for me that is fun, like a root canal or a hysterectomy.

I still say, "If God had wanted me to bend over, he would have sprinkle the floor with diamonds!"

Photos - EVERY DOG HAS HIS DAY

EVERY DOG HAS HIS DAY

PHOTOS - WHY PETS BIT PEOPLE and HATE HALLOWEEN

PHOTOS - WHY WOMEN DON'T MARRY

CELEBRITY MANSIONS

Lifestyles of the Rich and Famous...not sure which house goes with which name **EXCEPT the last home supposedly belongs to Miss Spears...** (other houses... Travolta, Winfrey, Spelling, Murphy, Smith, Stewart, Hefner, King, Pitt, Stallone, Seinfeld ?)

MORNING SMILE - KIDS!!

- **NUDITY** – I was driving with my 3 young children, one summer evening, when a woman in a convertible pulls up beside me. She was stark naked! As I was reeling from the shock, I heard my 5 year old shout from the back seat, "Mom, that lady isn't wearing a seat belt!"

- **OPINIONS** – On the first day of school, a first-grader handed his teacher a note from his mother. The note read, "The opinions expressed by this child are not necessarily those of his parents."

  - **KETCHUP** – A woman was trying hard to get the ketchup out of the bottle. During her struggle the phone rang, so she asked her 4 year old daughter to answer it. "Mommy can't come to the phone to talk to you right now. She's hitting the bottle."

  - **MORE NUDITY** – A little boy got lost at the YMCA and found himself in the women's locker room. When he was spotted, the room burst into shrieks with ladies grabbing towels and running for cover. The little boy watched in amazement and then asked, "What's the matter, haven't you ever seen a little boy before?"

- **POLICE** – While taking a routine vandalism report at an elementary school, I was interrupted by a little girl about 6 years old. Looking up and down at my uniform, she asked, "Are you a cop?" "Yes," I answered and continued writing my report. "My mother said if I ever needed help, I should ask the police. Is that right?" "Yes, that's right," I told her. "Well then," she said extending her foot toward me, "would you please tie my shoe?"

- **POLICE** – It was the end of the day when I parked my police van in front of the station. As I gathered my equipment my K-9 partner, Jake, was barking and I saw a little boy staring in at me. "Is that a dog you got back there?" he asked. "It sure is," I replied. Puzzled, the boy looked at me and then towards the back of the van. Finally he said, "What'd he do?"

- **ELDERLY** – While working for an organization that delivers lunches to elderly shut-ins, I took my 4 year old daughter on afternoon rounds. She was intrigued by the various appliances of old age, particularly the canes, walkers and wheelchairs. One day, I found her staring at a pair of false teeth soaking in a glass. As I braced myself for the inevitable barrage of questions, she merely turned and whispered, "The tooth fairy will never believe this!"

- **DRESS-UP** – A little girl was watching her parents dress for a party. When she saw her dad donning his tuxedo she warned, "Daddy, you shouldn't wear that suit." "Why not, darling?" "You know that it always gives you a headache the next morning."

- **DEATH** – While walking along the sidewalk, in front of his church, our minister heard the intoning of a prayer that nearly made his collar wilt. Apparently, his 5 year old son and his playmates had found a dead robin. Feeling that proper burial should be performed, they had secured a small box and cotton batting, then dug a hole and made ready for the disposal of the deceased. The minister's son was chosen to say the appropriate prayers and with sonorous dignity intoned his version of what he thought his father always said, "Glory be unto the Faaather and unto the Sonnn and in the hole he Goooes."

- **SCHOOL** – A little girl had just finished her first week of school. "I'm just wasting my time," she said to her mother. "I can't read, I can't write and they won't let me talk!"

- **BIBLE** – A little boy opened the big family Bible. He was fascinated as he fingered through the old pages. Suddenly, something fell out of the Bible. He picked up the object and looked at it. "Mama, look what I found," the boy called out. "What have you got there, dear?" With astonishment in the young boy's voice he answered, "I think its Adam's underwear."

VALUE OF MATURE WOMEN (Andy Rooney)

As I grow in age, I value women over 40 most of all. Here are just a few reasons why:

- A woman over 40 will never wake you in the middle of the night and ask, "What are you thinking?" She doesn't care what you think.
- If a woman over 40 doesn't want to watch the game, she doesn't sit around whining about it. She does something she wants to do, and it's usually more interesting.
- Women over 40 are dignified. They seldom have a screaming match with you at the opera or in the middle of an expensive restaurant. Of course, if you deserve it, they won't hesitate to shoot you if they think they can get away with it.
- Older women are generous with praise, often undeserved. They know what it's like to be unappreciated.
- Women get psychic as they age.
- You never have to confess your sins to a woman over 40.
- Once you get past a wrinkle or two, a woman over 40 is far sexier than her younger counterpart.
- Older women are forthright and honest. They'll tell you right off the bat if you're a jerk or if you're acting like one. You don't ever have to wonder where you stand with her!

Yes, we praise women over 40 for a multitude of reasons. Unfortunately, it's not reciprocal. For every stunning, smart, well-coiffed, hot woman over 40, there is a bald, paunchy relic in yellow pants making a fool of himself with some 22 year old waitress. Ladies, I apologize. For all those men who say, "Why buy the cow when you can get the milk for free?" Here's an update. Now-a-days, 80% of women are against marriage. Why? **Because women realize it's not worth buying an entire pig just to get a little sausage!**

BLONDE - RIVER

Janice, a blonde, is out for a walk. She comes to a river and sees another blonde, Tish, on the opposite bank. "Yoo-hoo!" Janice shouts, "How can I get to the other side?" Tish looks up the river then down the river and shouts back, "You ARE on the other side!"

COSTUME PARTY

A Couple was invited to a swanky costume party. Karen got a terrible headache and told her husband, Ric, to go to the party alone. Ric, being a devoted husband protested, but Karen argued and said she was going to take some aspirin and go to bed. There was no need of his good time being spoiled by not going. So Ric took his costume and away he went. Karen, after sleeping soundly for about an hour, awakened without pain and decided to go to the party, as it was still early. Since Ric did not know what her costume was, Karen thought she would have some fun by watching Ric to see how he acted when she was not with him. Karen joined the party and soon spotted Ric cavorting around on the dance floor, dancing with every nice chick he could, copping a little feel here and a little kiss there. Karen slithered up to him and, being a rather seductive babe herself, he left his current partner high and dry and devoted his time to the new babe that had just arrived. Karen let Ric go as far as he wished, naturally, since he was her husband. Finally, he whispered a little proposition in her ear and she agreed, so off they went to one of the cars and had a little bang. Just before unmasking at midnight, Karen slipped away, went home, put the costume away and got into bed wondering what kind of explanation Ric would make for his behavior.

Karen was sitting up reading when Ric came in and she asked what kind of a time he had. Ric said, "Oh, the same old thing. You know I never have a good time when you're not there." "Did you dance much?" "I'll tell you, I never even danced one dance. When I got there, I met David, Roy, Kevin and some other guys, so we went into the den and played poker all evening. But you're not going to believe what happened to the guy who borrowed my costume!"

203

THE MORTICIAN

A man who just died is delivered to a Louisiana mortuary wearing an expensive, expertly tailored black suit. Boudreaux, the mortician, asks the deceased's wife how she would like the body dressed. He points out that the man does look very good in the black suit he is already wearing. The widow, however, says that she always thought her husband, Martin, looked best in blue and that she wants him in a blue suit.

She gives Boudreaux a blank check and says, "I don't care what it costs, just have my husband in a blue suit for the viewing." The woman returns the next day for the viewing. To her delight, she finds her husband dressed in a gorgeous blue suit with a subtle chalk stripe; the suit fits him perfectly. She says to Boudreaux, "Whatever the suit cost, I'm very satisfied. You did an excellent job and I'm very grateful. How much did you spend?"

To her astonishment, Boudreaux presents her with a blank check. "There's no charge," he says. "No, really, I must pay you for the cost of that exquisite blue suit!" she says. "Honestly, ma'am," Boudreaux says, "It didn't cost me a thing. You see, a deceased gentleman, of about your husband's size, was brought in shortly after you left yesterday and he was wearing an attractive blue suit. I asked his missus if she minded him going to his grave wearing a black suit instead and she said it made no difference as long as he looked nice." "So, I just switched the heads."

BLONDE - REDHEAD

A gorgeous young redhead goes into the doctor's office and said that her body hurt whenever she touched it. "Impossible!" says the doctor. "Show me." The redhead took her finger, pushed on her left shoulder and screamed, and then she pushed her elbow and screamed even more. She pushed her knee and screamed; likewise she pushed her head and screamed. Everywhere she touched made her scream. The doctor said, "You're not really a redhead, are you?" "Well, no," she said, "I'm actually a blonde." "I thought so," the doctor said. "Your finger is broken."

GRANDPA

There was a family gathering with all generations around the table. Mischievous teenagers put a Viagra tablet into Grandpa's drink and after a while, Grandpa excused himself because he had to go to the bathroom. When he returned, however, his trousers were wet all over. "What happened, Grandpa?" asked his concerned children.

"Well," he answered, "I don't really know, I had to go to the bathroom, so I took it out and started to pee, but then I saw that it wasn't mine so I put it back."

WE ALL NEED A TREE

I hired a plumber to help me restore an old farmhouse and after he had just finished a rough first day on the job, a flat tire made him lose an hour of work, his electric drill quit and his ancient, one ton truck refused to start. While I drove him home, he sat in stony silence. On arriving, he invited me in to meet his family. As we walked toward the front door, he paused briefly at a small tree, touching the tips of the branches with both hands. While opening the door, he underwent an amazing transformation. His face was wreathed in smiles; he hugged his two small children and gave his wife a kiss. Afterward, he walked me to the car. We passed the tree and my curiosity got the best of me. I asked him about what I had seen earlier. "Oh, that's my trouble tree," he replied. "I know I can't help having troubles on the job, but one thing's for sure, those troubles don't belong in the house with my wife and children, so I just hang them up on the tree every night when I come home, and ask God to take care of them. Then in the morning, I pick them up again." "Funny thing is," he smiled, "when I come out in the morning to pick 'em up, there aren't nearly as many as I remember hanging up the night before." We All Need a Tree!!!

GEOGRAPHY OF A WOMAN

- Between 18 and 22, a woman is like AFRICA – Half discovered, half wild and naturally beautiful with fertile soil.
- Between 23 and 30, a woman is like **AMERICA** – Well developed and open to trade, especially for someone with cash.
- Between 31 and 35, a woman is like INDIA – Very hot, relaxed and convinced of her own beauty.
- Between 36 and 40, a woman is like **FRANCE** – Gently aging, but still a warm and desirable place to visit.
- Between 41 and 50, a woman is like **GREAT BRITAIN** – With a glorious and all conquering past.
- Between 51 and 60, a woman is like **YUGOSLAVIA** – Lost some wars, won some great battles but haunted by past mistakes; still very strong and proud.
- Between 61 and 70, a woman is like **RUSSIA** – Very wide and borders are now largely unpatrolled.
- After 70, she becomes TIBET – Off the beaten path with a mysterious past and the wisdom of the ages; still desirable, but only those with an adventurous spirit and a thirst for spiritual knowledge and true love dare visit there.

GEOGRAPHY OF A MAN
- Between 1 and 78, a man is like **IRAN** – Ruled by a dick.

WISDOM OF THE HEART

Be kind whenever possible. It's always possible. Open your arms to change but don't let go of your values. Sleep is the best meditation. Spend some time alone every day. We can never obtain peace in the outer world until we make peace with ourselves. The root of all goodness lies in the soil of appreciation for goodness. We can live without religion and meditation, but we cannot survive without human affection. Happiness is not something 'ready made'. It comes from your own actions. If you can, help others; if you cannot do that, at least do not harm them. The ultimate authority must always rest with the individual's own reason and critical analysis.

Do THE DISHES

Joe wanted to buy a motorcycle. He doesn't have much luck until, one day, he comes across a Harley with a 'for sale' sign on it. The bike seems even better than a new one, although it's 10 years old. It's shinny and in absolute mint condition. He immediately buys it and asks the seller how he kept it in such great condition for 10 years. "Well, it's really quite simple," says the seller, "whenever the bike is outside and it's going to rain, I rub Vaseline on the chrome. It protects it from the rain." He hands Joe a jar of Vaseline.

That night his girlfriend, Sandra, invites him over to meet her parents. Naturally, they take the bike. Just before they enter the house, Sandra stops him and says, "I have to tell you something about my family before we go in. When we eat dinner, we don't talk. In fact, the first person who says anything during dinner has to do the dishes." "No problem," he says and they go in. Joe is shocked. Right smack in the middle of the living room is a huge stack of dirty dishes. In the kitchen is another huge stack of dishes. Piled up on the stairs, in the corridor and everywhere he looks are dirty dishes. They sit down and sure enough no one says a word.

As dinner progresses, Joe decides to take advantage of the situation and leans over and kisses Sandra. No one says a word so he reaches over and fondles her breasts. Still, nobody says a word. He stands up, grabs her, rips her clothes off, throws her on the table and screws her right there, in front of her parents. His girlfriend is a little flustered, her dad is obviously livid and her mom is horrified when he sits back down, but no one says a word. He looks at her mom. "She's got a great body," he thinks, so he grabs the mom, bends her over the dinner table and has his way with her every which way, right there on the dinner table. Now his girlfriend is furious and her dad is boiling, but still, total silence. All of a sudden, there is a loud clap of thunder and it starts to rain. Joe remembers his bike, so he pulls the jar of Vaseline from his pocket. Suddenly, the father backs away from the table and shouts, "Alright, alright, I'll do the flipping dishes!"

LUCKY MAN IN N.Y.

A New York man retired and decided to buy a home with a few acres in Portugal. The modest farmhouse had been vacant for 15 years; the owner and wife both had died and there were no heirs. The house was sold to pay taxes. There had been several lookers, but the large barn had steel doors and they had been wired shut. Nobody wanted to go the extra expense to see what was in the barn and it wasn't complimentary to the property, anyway, so nobody made an offer on the place. The NY guy bought it at just over half of the property's worth, moved in and set about to tear into the barn. Curiosity was killing him so he and his wife bought a generator and a couple of grinders and cut thru the weeds and this is what they found...

WET PANTS

Come with me to a third grade classroom… There is a nine year old kid sitting at his desk and all of a sudden, there is a puddle between his feet and the front of his pants are wet. He thinks his heart is going to stop because he cannot possibly imagine how this happened. It's never happened before and he knows that when the boys find out, he will never hear the end of it. When the girls find out, they'll never speak to him again as long as he lives.

The boy believes his heart is going to stop and he puts his head down and prays, "Dear God, this is an emergency! I need help now! Five minutes from now I'm dead meat."

He looks up from his prayer and here comes the teacher with a look in her eyes that says he has been discovered. As the teacher is walking toward him, a classmate, named Susie, is carrying a goldfish bowl that is filled with water. Susie trips in front of the teacher and inexplicably dumps a bowl of water in the boy's lap. The boy pretends to be angry, but all the while is saying to himself, "Thank you, Lord! Thank you!"

Now, all of a sudden, instead of being the object of ridicule the boy is the object of sympathy. The teacher rushes him downstairs and gives him gym shorts to put on while his pants dry out. All the other children are on their hands and knees cleaning up around his desk. The sympathy is wonderful. But as life would have it, the ridicule that should have been his, has been transferred to someone else, Susie. She tries to help, but they tell her to get out, "You've done enough, you klutz!"

Finally, at the end of the day, as they are waiting for the bus, the boy walks over to Susie and whispers, "You did that on purpose, didn't you?" Susie whispers back, **"I wet my pants once, too."**

209

NEW YORK GIRL

A girl from New York and a girl from the West Coast were seated side by side on an airplane. The girl from New York, being friendly and all, said, "So, where ya from?" The West Coast girl said, "From a place where they no better than to use a preposition at the end of a sentence." The girl from New York, sat quietly for a few moments and then replied, **"So, where ya from,** *bitch?"*

PHOTOS - REMEMBER in COLOR

SEVEN WONDERS OF THE WORLD

A group of students were asked to list what they thought were the present 'Seven Wonders of the World'. Though there was some disagreement, the following received the most votes:

1. Egypt's Great Pyramids
2. Taj Mahal
3. Grand Canyon
4. Panama Canal
5. Empire State Building
6. St. Peter's Basilica
7. China's Great Wall

While gathering the votes, the teacher noted one student had not finished her paper. So she asked the girl if she was having trouble with her list. The girl replied, "Yes, a little. I couldn't quite make my mind up because there are so many." The teacher said, "Well, tell us what you have and maybe we can help." The girl hesitated then read, "I think the Seven Wonders of the World are:"

1. To **SEE**
2. To **TOUCH**
3. To **FEEL**
4. To **HEAR**
5. To **TASTE**
6. To **LAUGH**
7. To **LOVE**

BLONDE - VENTRILOQUIST

A young ventriloquist, Jason, is touring the clubs and one night he's doing a show in a small town in Arkansas. With his dummy on his knee, Jason starts going through his usual routine of telling dumb blonde jokes. Suddenly a blonde woman in the 4th row stands on her chair and starts shouting, "I've heard enough of your stupid blonde jokes. What makes you think you can stereotype women that way? What does the color of a person's hair have to do with her worth as a human being?" "Its guys like you who keep women like me from being respected at work and in the community and from reaching our full potential as a person. Because you and your kind continue to perpetuate discrimination against, not only blondes but women in general, and all in the name of humor!" Embarrassed, Jason begins to apologize and the blonde yells, "You stay out of this, mister! I'm talking to that little s*** on your knee!"

211

THE GENIE

A husband takes his wife to play her first game of golf. Of course, the wife promptly whacked her first shot right through the window of the biggest house adjacent to the course. The husband cringed, "I warned you to be careful! Now we'll have to go up there, find the owner, apologize and see how much your lousy drive is going to cost us." So the couple walked up to the house and knocked on the door. A warm voice said, "Come in." When they opened the door, they saw the damage that was done; glass was all over the place and a broken antique bottle was lying on its side near the broken window. A man reclining on the couch asked, "Are you the people that broke my window?" "Uh, yeah, sir. We're sure sorry about that," the husband replied. "Oh, no apology is necessary. Actually I want to thank you; you see, I'm a genie and I've been trapped in that bottle for a thousand years. Now that you've released me, I'm allowed to grant three wishes. I'll give you each one wish, but if you don't mind, I'll keep the last one for myself."

"Wow, that's great!" the husband said. He pondered a moment and blurted out, "I'd like a million dollars a year for the rest of my life!" "No problem," said the genie. "You've got it, it's the least I can do and I'll guarantee you a long, healthy life." "And now you, young lady, what do you want?" the genie asked. "I'd like to own a gorgeous home, complete with servants, in every country in the world," she said. "Consider it done," the genie said, "And your homes will always be safe from fire, burglary and natural disasters." "And now," the couple asked in unison, what's your wish, genie?" "Well, since I've been trapped in that bottle and haven't been with a woman in more than a thousand years, my wish is to have sex with your wife." The husband looked at his wife and said, "Gee, honey, you know now that we both have a fortune and all those houses, what do you think?" She mulled it over for a few moments and said, "You know, you're right. Considering our good fortune, I guess I wouldn't mind, but what about you, honey?" "You know I love you, sweetheart," said the husband. "I'd do the same for you."

So the genie and the woman went upstairs, where they spent the rest of the afternoon enjoying each other in every way. After about three hours of non-stop sex, the genie rolled over and looked directly into her eyes and asked, "How old are you and your husband?" "Why, we're both 35," she responded breathlessly. "No S***," he said, "Thirty-five years old and both of you **still believe in genies**?"

212

PHOTOS - FOOD IN FOREIGN COUNTRIES

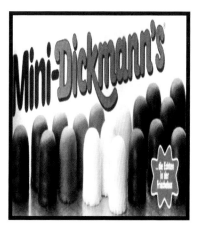

THE MUSLIM QUARTERBACK

The Coach had put together the perfect team for the Oakland Raiders. The only thing missing was a good quarterback. He had scouted all the colleges and even the Canadian and European Leagues, but he couldn't find a ringer who could ensure a Super Bowl victory. Then one night, while watching CNN, he saw a war-zone scene in Afghanistan. In one corner of the background he spotted a young Afghan-Muslim soldier with a truly incredible arm. He threw a grenade from 50 yards down a chimney and then hit a passing car going 80 miles per hour. "I've got to get this guy!" Coach said to himself. "He has the perfect arm!" So he brings the young Afghan to the States, teaches him the great game of football and, sure enough, the Raiders go on to win the Super Bowl.

The young Afghan is hailed as a hero of football and when the Coach asks him what he wants, all the young man wants to do is call his mother. "Mom," he says into the phone, "I just won the Super Bowl!" "I don't want to talk to you," the old Muslim woman says. "You have disappointed us. You are not my son!" "Mother, I don't think you understand," pleads the son, "I've just won the greatest sporting event in the world!" "No! Let me tell you," his mother retorts, "At this very moment, there are gunshots all around us. The neighborhood is a pile of rubble. Your two brothers were beaten within an inch of their lives last week and I have to keep your sister in the house so she doesn't get assaulted!" The old lady pauses, and then tearfully says, **"I will never forgive you for making us move to Oakland!"**

HOW THE FIGHT STARTED

I rear-ended a car this morning. So there we were along the road and slowly the driver gets out of the car and you know how you just get *sooo* stressed and life-stuff seems to get funny? Yeah, well, I could NOT believe it...he was a DWARF! He storms over to my car, looks up at me and says, "I AM NOT HAPPY!" So I look down at him and simply say, **"Well, which one are you then?"**

And that's when the fight started...

ILLEGALS

The L.A. Times published the following data:

- 40% of all workers in L.A. County (L.A. County has 10.2 million people) are working for cash and not paying taxes. This is because they are predominantly illegal immigrants working without a green card.

- 95% of warrants for murder in Los Angeles are for illegal aliens.

- 75% of people on the most wanted list in Los Angeles are illegal aliens.

- Over 2/3 of all births in L.A. County are illegal alien Mexicans on Medicare, whose births were paid for by taxpayers.

- Nearly 35% of all inmates in California detention centers are Mexicans, here illegally.

- Over 300,000 illegal aliens in L.A. County are living in garages.

- The FBI reports half of all gang members in L.A. County are, most likely, illegal aliens from south of the border.

- Nearly 60% of all occupants of HUD properties are illegal.

- 21 radio stations in L.A. are Spanish speaking.

- In L.A. County, 5.1 million people speak English, 3.9 million speak Spanish. (There are 10.2 million people in L.A…so what's the rest??).

- Less than 2% of illegal aliens are picking our crops, but 29% are on welfare.

- Over 70% of the United States' annual population growth (and over 90% of California, Florida and New York) results from immigration.

SEVEN KINDS OF SEX

1. **Smurf** Sex. This kind of sex happens when you first meet someone and you both have sex until you are blue in the face.
2. **Kitchen** Sex. This is when you have been with your partner for a short time and you are so horny you will have sex anywhere, even in the kitchen.
3. **Bedroom** Sex. This is when you have been with your partner for a long time. Your sex has gotten routine and you usually have sex only in your bedroom.
4. **Hallway** Sex. This is when you have been with your partner for too long. When you pass each other in the hallway, you both say, "Screw you."
5. **Religious** Sex. This means you get Nun in the morning, Nun in the afternoon and Nun at night.
6. **Courtroom** Sex. This is when you cannot stand your partner anymore. He/She takes you to court and screws you in front of everyone.
7. **Social Security** Sex. You get a little each month but not enough to live on.

FLIGHT ATTENDANTS REPLACED

Replace all female flight attendants with good looking strippers. What the hell? The attendants have gotten old and haggard looking. They don't even serve food anymore, so what's the loss? The stripper would double, triple, perhaps quadruple the alcohol consumption and get a 'party atmosphere' going in the cabin. Muslims would be afraid to get on the planes for fear of seeing a naked woman. And, of course, every heterosexual businessman in this country would start flying again hoping to see naked women. Hijackings would come to a screeching halt and the airline industry would see record revenue. Why the hell didn't Bush think of this? Why do I still have to do everything myself?

Sincerely,
Bill Clinton

216

POEM - AIRPORT COOKIES

At an airport one night, with several long hours before her flight,
She hunted for a book in an airport shop, bought a bag of cookies and found a place to drop.
She was engrossed in her book, but happened to see that the man sitting beside her, as bold as could be, grabbed a cookie or two from the bag in between, which she tried to ignore to avoid a scene.
So she munched the cookies and watched the clock, as the gusty cookie thief diminished her stock.
She was getting more irritated as the minutes ticked by, thinking, "If I wasn't so nice, I would blacken his eye."
With each cookie she took, he took one too. When only one was left, she wondered what he would do. With a smile on his face, and a nervous laugh, he took the last cookie and broke it in half.
He offered her half, as he ate the other; she snatched it from him and thought...ooh, brother! This guy had some nerve and he's also rude.
Why he didn't even show any gratitude!
She had never known when she'd been so galled and sighed with relief when her flight was called. She gathered her belongings and headed to the gate, refusing to look back at the thieving ingrate.
She boarded the plane and sank in her seat, and then she sought her book, which was almost complete.
As she reached in her bag she gasped with surprise; there was her bag of cookies, in front of her eyes.
If mine are here, she moaned in despair, the others were his and he tried to share.
Too late to apologize, she realized with grief that she was the rude one; the ingrate, the thief!

How many times have we absolutely known that something was a certain way, only to discover later that what we believed to be true was not? Always keep an open mind and an open heart because you just never know; you might be eating someone else's cookies.

2008 DEMOCRATIC NATIONAL CONVENTION

Schedule of events

- 7:00   pm – Opening Ceremonial Flag Burning
- 7:15   pm – Pledge of Allegiance to the United Nations
- 7:20   pm – Ted Kennedy proposes a toast
- 7:25   pm – Nonreligious Prayer and Worship with Jesse Jackson & Al Sharpton
- 7:45   pm – Ceremonial Tree Hugging
- 7:55   pm – Ted Kennedy proposes a toast
- 8:00   pm – How I Invented the Internet – Al Gore
- 8:15   pm – Gay Wedding Planning – Barney Frank Presiding
- 8:35   pm – Ted Kennedy proposes a toast
- 8:40   pm – Our Troops are War Criminals – John Kerry
- 9:00   pm – Memorial Service for Saddam and His Sons – Cindy Sheehan & Susan Sarandon
- 10:00   pm – Answering Machine Etiquette – Alec Baldwin
- 11:00   pm – Ted Kennedy proposes a toast
- 11:05   pm – Collection for the Osama Bin Laden Kidney Transplant Fund – Barbara Streisand
- 11:15   pm – Free the Freedom Fighters from Guantanamo Bay – Sean Penn
- 11:30   pm – Oval Office Affairs – Bill Clinton
- 11:45   pm – Ted Kennedy proposes a toast
- 11:50   pm – How George Bush Brought Down the World Trade Towers – Howard Dean
- 12:15   am – Truth in Broadcasting Award – Presented to Dan Rather by Michael Moore
- 12:25   am – Ted Kennedy proposes a toast
- 12:30   am – Satellite Address by Mahmoud Ahmadinejad
- 12:45   am – Nomination of Hillary Rodham Clinton by Nancy Pelosi
- 1:00   am – Ted Kennedy proposes a toast
- 1:05   am – Coronation of Hillary Rodham Clinton
- 1:30   am – Ted Kennedy proposes a toast
- 1:35   am – **Bill Clinton asks Ted Kennedy to drive Hillary home**

FIRST JOB

A young family moved into a house next to a vacant lot. One day, a construction crew turned up to start building a house on the empty lot. The young family's 5 year old daughter naturally took an interest in all the activity going on next door and spent much of each day observing the workers. Eventually the construction crew, all of them 'gems-in-the-rough', more or less adopted her as a kind of project mascot. They chatted with her, let her sit with them while they had coffee and lunch breaks and gave her little jobs to do here and there to make her feel important. At the end of the first week they even presented her with a pay envelope containing ten dollars.

The little girl took this home to her mother, who suggested that she take her ten dollars 'pay' she'd received to the bank the next day to start a savings account. When the girl and her mom got to the bank, the teller was equally impressed and asked the little girl how she had come by her very own pay check at such a young age. The little girl proudly replied, "I worked last week with a real construction crew building the new house next door to us." "Oh my goodness gracious," said the teller, "And will you be working on the same house again this week, too?" The little girl replied, "I will if those a**holes at the Home Depot ever deliver the f-ing sheet rock."

OOPS!

A guy goes to the supermarket and notices and attractive woman waving at him. She says, "Hello." He's rather taken aback because he can't place where he knows her from. So he says, "Do you know me?" To which she replies, "I think you're the father of one of my kids." Now his mind travels back to the only time he has ever been unfaithful to his wife and says, "My God, are you the stripper from my bachelor party that I made love to on the pool table with all my buddies watching while your partner whipped my but with wet celery?" She looks into his eyes and says calmly, "No, I'm your son's teacher."

219

A LITTLE HISTORY LESSON

If you don't know the answer, take your best guest. Answer the questions before looking at the answers. **Who said it?**

- "We're going to take things away from you on behalf of the common good."
    - **A)** Karl Marx **B)** Adolph Hitler
    - **C)** Joseph Stalin **D)** None of the above

- "It's time for a new beginning, for an end to government of the few, by the few and for the few; and to replace it with shared responsibility for shared prosperity."
    - **A)** Lenin **B)** Mussolini
    - **C)** Idi Amin **D)** None of the above

- "We can't just let business as usual go on, and that means something has to be taken away from some people."
    - **A)** Nikita Khrushev **B)** Josef Goebbels
    - **C)** Boris Yeltsin **D)** None of the above

- "We have to build a political consensus and that requires people to give up a little bit of their own in order to create this common ground"
    - **A)** Mao Tse Dung **B)** Hugo Chavez
    - **C)** Kim Jong II **D)** None of the above

- "I certainly think the free-market has failed."
    - **A)** Karl Marx **B)** Lenin
    - **C)** Molotov **D)** None of the above

- "I think it's time to send a clear message to what has become the most profitable sector in the entire economy that they are being watched."
    - **A)** Pinochet **B)** Milosevic
    - **C)** Saddam Hussein **D)** None of the above

Answers:
All answers are 'D)' None of the above. All statements were made by Hillary Clinton

BE AFRAID, BE VERY AFRAID!!!

220

SEARS

I knew I needed this reminder, since Sears isn't always my first choice. It's amazing when you think of how long the war has lasted and they haven't withdrawn from their commitment. Could we each buy at least one thing at Sears this year? How does Sears treat its employees who are called up for military duty? By law, they are required to hold their jobs open and available, but nothing more. Usually, people take a big pay cut and lose benefits as a result of being called up. Sears is voluntarily paying the difference in salaries and maintaining all benefits, including medical insurance and bonus program for all called up reservist employees for up to two years. I submit that Sears is an exemplary corporate citizen and should be recognized for its contributions. I suggest we all shop at Sears and be sure to find a manager to tell them why we are there so the company gets the positive reinforcement it well deserves. I decided to check into this before I sent it forward.

I sent this email to the Sears Customer Service Department: I received this email and would like to know if it is true. If it is, the internet may have just become one very good source of advertisement for you company. I know I would go out of my way to buy products from Sears instead of another for a like item, even if it's cheaper at another store.

This was their answer to the email:

Dear Customer:

Thank you for contacting Sears. The information is factual. We appreciate your positive feedback. Sears regards service to our country as one of the greatest sacrifices our young men and women can make. We are happy to do our part to lessen the burden they bear at this time.

Sincerely,   Sears Customer Care

CARTOONS - EASTER

SHAMUS AND MURPHY

Shamus and Murphy fancied a pint or two but didn't have a lot of money between them. They could only raise the staggering sum of one Euro. Murphy said, "Hang on, I have an idea." He went next door to the butcher's shop and came out with one large sausage. Shamus said, "Are you crazy? Now we don't have any money left at all!" Murphy replied, "Don't worry just follow me." He went into the pub where he immediately ordered two pints of Guinness and two glasses of Jamieson. Shamus said, "Now you've lost it! Do you know how much trouble we'll be in? We haven't got any money!" Murphy replied with a smile, "Don't worry, I have a plan, Cheers!" They downed their drinks and Murphy said, "OK, I'll stick the sausage through my zipper and then you go on your knees and put it in your mouth." The bartender noticed them, went berserk and threw them out. They continued this act pub after pub, getting more and more drunk, all for free. At the tenth pub Shamus said, "Murphy, I don't think I can do any more of this. I'm drunk and my knees are killin' me!" Murphy said, "How do you think I feel? I lost the sausage at the third pub!"

OLDER LADY HUMOR

The next time you see a little old lady with shaky hands you'll remember this story: A little old lady well into her eighties, slowly enters the front door of a  sex shop. Obviously very unstable on her feet, she wobbles the few feet across the store to the counter. Finally arriving at the counter and grabbing it for support, stuttering, she asks the sales clerk, "Dddooo youuuu hhhave dddddiillllldosss?" The clerk, politely trying not to burst out laughing, replies, "Yes, we do have dildos. Actually we carry many different models." The old woman then asks, "Dddddoooo yyyouuuu ccaarrryy aaa pppinkk onnee, tttenn inchessss lllong aaandd aabbooutt ttwoo inchesss ththiick aaannd rrunns by bbaatteries?" The clerk responds, "Yes, we do." She asks, "Ddddooo yyoooouuuu kknnnoooww hhhowww tttooo ttturrrnnn ttthe ssuno ooffabbitch offfff?"

PHOTOS - FRIENDS

WORLD'S SHORTEST FAIRYTALE

Once upon a time, a girl asked a guy, "Will you marry me?"
The guy said, "No." And the girl lived happily ever after. She went shopping, drank martinis with friends, always had a clean house, never had to cook, had a closet full of shoes and handbags, stayed skinny and was never farted on. **THE END.**

An HONEST PRIEST

A distinguished young woman on a flight from Ireland asked the Priest beside her, "Father, may I ask a favor?" "Of course. What may I do for you?" "Well, I bought an expensive woman's electronic hair dryer for my mother's birthday that is unopened and well over the customs limits and I'm afraid they'll confiscate it. Is there any way you could carry it through Customs for me? Under your robes perhaps?" "I will help you, dear, but I must warn you, I will not lie." "With your honest face, Father, no one will question you." When they got to Customs, she let the priest go ahead of her. The official asked, "Father, do you have anything to declare?" "From the top of my head down to my waist, I have nothing to declare." The official thought this answer strange, so asked, "And what do you have to declare from your waist to the floor?" "I have a marvelous instrument designed to be used on a woman but, to date, is unused." Roaring with laughter, the official said, "Go ahead, Father. Next!"

Skinny DIPPIN'

An older man in California, Howard, had owned a large farm for several years. He had a large pond in the back. It was properly shaped for swimming, so he fixed it up nice; picnic tables, horseshoe pits and some apple and peach trees. One evening the old farmer decided to go down to the pond and look it over, as he hadn't been there in a while. Howard grabbed a five-gallon bucket to bring back some fruit. As he neared the pond, he heard voices shouting and laughing with glee. As he got closer he saw it was a bunch of young women skinny-dipping in his pond. He made the women aware of his presence and they all went to the deep end. One of the women shouted at him, "We're not coming out until you leave!" Howard frowned, "I didn't come down here to watch you ladies swim naked or make you get out of the pond naked." Holding the bucket up he said, "I'm here to feed the alligators!"

MAYA ANGELOU

In April, Maya Angelou was interviewed by Oprah on her 70th birthday. Oprah asked her what she thought of growing older, and there on television, she said it was 'Exciting'. Regarding body changes, she said there were many occurring every day, like her breasts. They seem to be in a race to see which will reach her waist first. The audience laughed so hard, they cried. She is such a simple and honest woman with so much wisdom in her words. Mary Angelou said this:

- "I've learned that no matter what happens, or how bad it seems today, life does go on and it will be better tomorrow."
- "I've learned that you can tell a lot about a person by the way he/she handles these three things: a rainy day, lost luggage and tangled Christmas tree lights."
- "I've learned regardless of your relationship with your parents, you'll miss them when they're gone from your life."
- "I've learned that making a 'living' is not the same thing as 'making a life'."
- "I've learned that life sometimes gives you a second chance."
- "I've learned that you shouldn't go through life with a catcher's mitt on both hands, you need to be able to throw some things back."
- "I've learned that whenever I decide something with an open heart, I usually make the right decision."
- "I've learned that even when I have pains, I don't have to be one."
- "I've learned that every day you should reach out and touch someone. People love a warm hug or just a friendly pat on the back."
- "I've learned that people will forget what you said, people will forget what you did, but people will never forget how you made them feel."

DEMOGRAPHICS YOU CAN RELATE TO

If we could reduce the world's population to a village of precisely 100 people, with all existing human ratios remaining the same, the demographics would look something like this:

- 56 Asian, 12 European, 5 American, 5 Canadian, 8 Latin, 14 African
- 49 would be female, 51 would be male
- 82 would be non-white, 18 white
- 89 heterosexual, 11 homosexual
- 33 would be Christian, 67 would be non-Christian
- 80 would live in substandard housing
- 24 would not have electricity
- 67 would be unable to read
- 50 would be malnourished, 1 dying of starvation
- 33 would be without access to safe water

If you woke up this morning with more health than sickness, you are luckier than the million that will not survive this week.

If you are able to go to church, mosque or synagogue without fear of harassment, arrest, torture or death, you are happier than 3 billion persons in this world.

If you are dressed and have got shoes, a meal in your refrigerator, a bed and a roof above your head, you are better off than 75% of people in this world.

If your parents are still alive and still married, you are a rarity.

MESSAGE OF THE DAY

When you're having a bad day and it seems like people are actually trying to make you angry, remember, it takes 42 muscles to frown but only 4 muscles to pull the trigger of a decent sniper rifle. Remember, when someone annoys you it takes 42 muscles in your face to frown BUT it only takes 4 muscles to extend your arm and bitch-slap the f****r upside the head.

226

Miracle of Toilet Paper

Fresh from my shower I was standing in front of the mirror complaining to my husband that my breasts are too small. Instead of characteristically telling me it's no so bad, he uncharacteristically comes up with a suggestion. "If you want your breasts to grow, then every day take a piece of toilet paper and rub it between them for a few seconds. They will grow larger over a period of years." My husband replies. I fetch a piece of toilet paper and stand in front of the mirror, looking at it and looking at my breasts. "Do you really think rubbing a piece of toilet paper between my breasts everyday will make my breasts larger over the years?" Without missing a beat, he says, **"It worked for your butt, didn't it?"** He's still alive and with a great deal of therapy, he may even walk again some day. Stupid, stupid man!

Little Justin and Jenny

Little Justin and Jenny are only 10 years old, but know that they are in love. One day they decide that they want to get married, so Justin goes to Jenny's father to ask him for her hand. Justin bravely walks up to him and says, "Mr. Smith, me and Jenny are in love and I want to ask you for her hand in marriage." Thinking this was just the cutest thing, Mr. Smith replies, "Well Justin, you are only 10. Where will you two live?" Without even taking a moment to think about it, Bruce replies, "In Jenny's room. It's bigger than mine and we can both fit there nicely." Still thinking this is just adorable, Mr. Smith says, with a huge grin, "Okay then, how will you live? You're not old enough to get a job. You'll need to support Jenny." Again, Justin instantly replies, "Our allowance. Jenny makes 5 bucks a week and I make 10 bucks a week. That's about 60 bucks a month and that should do us just fine." By this time, Mr. Smith is a little shocked that Justin has put so much thought into this. He thinks for a moment trying to come up with something that Justin won't have an answer to. After a second, Mr. Smith says, "Well Justin, it seems like you have got everything all figured out. I just have one more question for you, "What will you do if the two of you should have little ones of your own?" Justin just shrugs his shoulders and says, "Well, we've been lucky so far." Mr. Smith no longer thinks the little s*** is so adorable.

THE SEX FAIRY

- Sex is a beauty treatment. Scientific tests find that when women make love they produce amounts of estrogen, which makes hair shine and their skin smooth.

  Gentle, relaxed lovemaking reduces your chances of suffering dermatitis, skin rashes and blemishes. The sweat produced cleanses the pores and makes your skin glow.

- Lovemaking can burn up those calories you piled on during that romantic dinner.

- Sex is one of the safest sports you can take up. It stretches and tones just about every muscle in the body. It's more enjoyable than swimming 20 laps and you don't need special sneakers!

- Sex is an instant cure for mild depression. It releases endorphins into the bloodstream producing a sense of euphoria and leaves you with a feeling of well-being.

- The more sex you have, the more you may be offered. The sexually active body gives off greater quantities of chemicals called pheromones. These subtle sex perfumes drive the opposite sex crazy!

- Sex is the safest tranquilizer in the world. It's 10 times more effective than Valium.

- Kissing each day will keep the dentist away. Kissing encourages saliva to wash food from the teeth and lowers the level of the acid that causes decay, preventing plaque build-up.

- Sex actually relieves headaches. A lovemaking session can release the tension that restricts blood vessels in the brain.

- A lot of lovemaking can unblock a stuffy nose. Sex is a natural antihistamine. It can help combat asthma and hay fever.

- This message brings good luck for sex.

228

HOW QUICKLY TIME PASSES

CARJACKING - LADIES BEWARE

You walk across the parking lot, unlock your car and get inside. You start the engine and shift into reverse. When you look into the rearview mirror, to back out of your parking space, you notice a piece of paper stuck to the middle of the rear window. You shift into park, unlock your doors and jump out of your car to remove the paper, or whatever it is, that's obstructing your view. When you reach the back of your car that's when the car jackers appear out of nowhere, jump into your cal and take off. They practically mow you down as they speed off in your car. And guess what ladies? I bet your purse is still in the car. So now the carjacker has your car, your home address, your money and your keys. Your home and your whole identity are now compromised! **Beware!!!**

229

(Gwen, we're okay on the 'blank page' cost. bjm)

CHAPTER 7

THAT's ALL FOLKS !!!

THE ACCOUNTANT

Larry, the accountant, gets home late one night and his wife, Linda, says, "Where have you been?" Larry replied, "I was out getting a tattoo." "A tattoo?" she frowned. "What kind of tattoo did you get?" "I got a hundred dollar bill on my privates," he said proudly. "What the hell are you thinking?" she said, shaking her head in disdain. "Why on earth would an accountant get a hundred dollar bill tattooed on his privates?" "Well, first, I like to watch my money grow. Second, once in a while I like to play with my money. Third, I like how money feels in my hand. Lastly, instead of you going out shopping, you can stay right here at home and blow a hundred bucks anytime you want."

SEX STUDY

It has been determined that the most used sexual position for married couples is the doggie position. The husband sits up and begs. The wife rolls over and plays dead.

THE CORK

Two Arab terrorists are in a locker room taking a shower after their bomb making class, when one notices the other has a huge cork stuck in his butt! "If you do not mind me saying," said the second, "That cork looks very uncomfortable. Why don't you take it out?" "I regret I cannot say," lamented the first Arab. "It is permanently stuck in my butt." "I do not understand," said the other. The first Arab says, "I was walking along the beach and I tripped over an oil lamp. There was a puff of smoke, and then a huge old man in American flag attire with a white beard and top hat came boiling out." He said, "I am Uncle Sam, the Genie. I can grant you one wish. He said, "...no s***?"

ITALIAN TOMATO GARDEN

An Old Italian man lived alone out in the country. He wanted to dig his tomato garden, but it was very hard work, as the ground was hard. His only son, Vincent, who used to help him, was in prison. The old man wrote a letter to his son and described his predicament.

Dear Vincent,
I am feeling pretty bad because it looks like I won't be able to plant my tomato garden this year. I'm just getting too old to be digging up a garden plot. I know if you were here, my troubles would be over. I know you would be happy to dig the plot for me.

Love, Dad

A few days later he received a letter from his son.

Dear Dad,
Don't dig up the garden. That's where I buried the bodies.

Love, Vinnie

At 4 a.m. the next morning FBI agents and local police arrived and dug up the entire area without finding any bodies. They apologized to the old man and left. That same day, the old man received another letter from his son.

Dear Dad,
Go ahead and plant the tomatoes now. That's the best I could do under the circumstances.

Love, Vinnie

233

MOTHER'S WISDOM

We should be grateful to our Mothers for teaching us the following:

- **APPRECIATE A JOB WELL DONE**
  "If you're going to kill each other, do it outside, I just finished cleaning."

- **RELIGION**
  "You better pray that will come out of the carpet."

- **TIME TRAVEL**
  "If you don't straighten up, I'm going to knock you into the middle of next week!"

- **LOGIC**
  "Because I said so, that's why."

- **MORE LOGIC**
  "If you fall out of that swing and break your neck, you're not going to the store with me."

- **FORESIGHT**
  "Make sure you wear clean underwear, in case you're in an accident."

- **IRONY**
  "Keep crying and I'll give you something to cry about!"

- **OSMOSIS**
  "Shut your mouth and eat your supper."

- **CONTORTIONISM**
  "Will you look at that dirt on the back of your neck?"

- **STAMINA**
  "You'll sit there until all that spinach is gone."

- **WEATHER**
  "This room of yours looks as if a tornado went through it."

- **HYPOCRISY**
  "If I told you once, I've told you a million times. Don't exaggerate!"

- **CIRCLE OF LIFE**
  "I brought you into this world, and I can take you out."

- **BEHAVIOR MODIFICATION** — "Stop acting like your father!"
- **ENVY** — "There are millions of less fortunate children in this world who don't have wonderful parents like you do."
- **ANTICIPATION** — "Just wait until we get home."
- **RECEIVING** — "You are going to get it when you get home!"
- **MEDICAL SCIENCE** — "If you don't stop crossing your eyes, they are going to get stuck that way.
- **ESP** — "Put your sweater on; don't you think I know how cold you are?"
- **HUMOR** — "When that lawn mower cuts off your toes, don't come running to me."
- **BECOMING AN ADULT** — "If you don't eat your vegetables, you'll never grow up."

- **GENETICS** — "You're just like you father."
- **ROOTS** — "Shut that door behind you. Do you think you were born in a barn?"
- **WISDOM** — "When you get to be my age, you'll understand.

AND OUR FAVORITE ONE...

- **JUSTICE** — **"One day you'll have kids, and I hope they turn out just like you!"**

JEWISH BRA

A Jewish man walked into the Lingerie Department of Macy's in New York. He tells the saleslady, "I would like a Jewish bra for my wife, size 34B." With a quizzical look, the saleslady asked, "What kind of bra?" He repeated, "A Jewish bra. She said to tell you that she wanted a Jewish bra and that you would know what she wanted." "Ah, now I remember," said the saleslady. "We don't get as many requests for them as we used to. Most of our customers lately want the Catholic bra, or the Salvation Army bra, or the Presbyterian bra." Confused, and a little flustered, the man asked, "So, what are the differences?" The saleslady responded, "It's all really quite simple. The Catholic bra supports the masses. The Salvation Army lifts up the fallen, and the Presbyterian bra keeps them staunch and upright." He mused on that information for a minute and said, "Hmm. I know I'll regret asking, but what does the Jewish bar do?" "Ah, the Jewish bra," she replied, "Makes mountains out of molehills."

AUNT KAREN

A teacher gave her fifth grade class an assignment: Get their parents to tell them a story with a moral at the end of it. The next day the kids came back and one by one began to tell their stories. "Tony, do you have a story to share?" "Yes ma'am. My daddy told me a story about my Aunt Karen. She was a pilot in Desert Storm and her plane got hit. She had to bail out over enemy territory and all she had was a flask of whiskey, a pistol and a survival knife. She drank the whiskey on the way down so it wouldn't break and then her parachute landed right in the middle of twenty enemy troops. She shot fifteen of them with the gun until she ran out of bullets, killed four more with the knife until the blade broke and then she killed the last Iraqi with her hands."

"Good Heavens," said the horrified teacher. "What kind of moral did your daddy tell you from this horrible story?"

"Stay the hell away from Aunt Karen when she's been drinking!!!"

PHOTOS - MANDARIN AIRLINES

"Ladies and gentlemen, this is the captain speaking. First, we would like to thank you for choosing to fly Mandarin Airlines. As we taxi out to the runway please make yourself comfortable... and for those of you sitting on the right side of the plane, **please look to your LEFT.**"

PHOTOS - ANIMAL FRIENDS

BABY BOOMER MEMORIES

Another goody for the old-timers:

- My mom used to cut chicken, chop eggs and spread mayo on the same cutting board with the same knife and no bleach but we didn't seem to get food poisoning.
- My mom used to defrost hamburger on the counter *AND* I used to eat it raw sometimes, too.
- Our school sandwiches were wrapped in wax paper and were in a brown paper bag, not in ice pack coolers but I can't remember getting ecoli.

238

- Almost all of us would have rather gone swimming in the lake instead of a pristine pool (talk about boring), no beach closures then.
- The term cell phone would have conjured up a phone in a jail cell and a pager was the school PA system.
- We all took gym, not PE, and risked permanent injury with a pair of high top Ked's (only worn in gym) instead of having cross-training athletic shoes with air cushion soles and built in light reflectors. I can't recall any injuries but they must have happened because they tell us how much safer we are now.
- Flunking gym was not an option, even for stupid kids! I guess PE must be much harder than gym.
- Speaking of school, we all sang the national anthem, and staying in detention after school caught all sorts of negative attention.
- Remember school nurses? Ours wore a hat and everything.
- I thought that I was supposed to accomplish something before I was allowed to be proud of myself.
- I just can't recall how bored we were without computers, Play Station, Nintendo, X-box or 270 digital TV cable stations.
- Oh yeah, and where was the Benadryl and sterilization kit when I got that bee sting? I could have been killed!
- We played 'king of the hill' on piles of gravel left on vacant construction sites and when we got hurt, mom pulled out the 48-cent bottle of Mercurochrome (kids liked it better because it didn't sting like iodine did) and then we got spanked.
- Now it's a trip to the emergency room, followed by a 10-day dose of a $49 bottle of antibiotics. Mom calls the attorney to sue the contractor for leaving a horribly pile of gravel where it was such a threat.
- We didn't act up at the neighbor's house either, because if we did, we got our butt spanked and then when we got home we got our butt spanked again.
- To top it off, not a single person I knew had ever been told that they were from a dysfunctional family. How could we possibly have known that?
- Now we need to get into group therapy and anger management classes? We were obviously so duped by so many societal ills that we didn't notice the entire country wasn't taking Prozac! How did we ever survive???

239

CARTOONS - SILLY

PHOTOS - SILLY (a bad hair day) ! !

THE AMISH ELEVATOR

For the first time in their lives, an Amish boy and his father were in a big-city mall. They were amazed by almost everything they saw, especially by two shiny, silver walls that could move apart and then slide back together again. The boy asked, "What is this Father?" The father responded, "Son, I have never seen anything like this in my life. I don't know what it is." While the boy and his father were watching with amazement, a fat old lady, in a wheelchair moved up to the moving walls and pressed a button. The walls opened and the lady rolled between them into a small room. The walls closed and the boy and his father watched the small numbers above the walls light up sequentially. They continued to watch until it reached the last number and then the numbers began to light in the reverse order. Finally, the walls opened up again and a large-breasted gorgeous 24 year old blonde stepped out. The father, not taking his eyes off the young woman, said quietly to his son, **"Go get your mother."**

GEORGE AND MARY

Just because someone doesn't love you the way you want them to, doesn't mean they don't love you with all they have. George and Mary were both patients in a mental hospital. One day, while they were walking past the hospital pool, George suddenly jumped into the deep end. He sank to the bottom of the pool and stayed there. Mary promptly jumped in to save him. She swam to the bottom and pulled him out. When the Head Nurse Director became aware of Mary's heroic act, she immediately ordered her to be discharged from the hospital, as she now considered her to be mentally stable. When she went to tell Mary the news she said, "Mary, I have good news and bad news. The good news is you're being discharged, since you were able to rationally respond to a crisis by jumping in and saving the life of the person you love. I have concluded that your act displays sound mindedness. The bad news is George hung himself in the bathroom with his bathrobe belt right after you saved him. I am so sorry, but he's dead."

Mary replied, "He didn't hang himself, I put him there to dry. How soon can I go home?"

PROVERBS #2 (Thank you Mr. LaRusso)

- Old friends, like old wines, don't lose their flavor.
- When you teach your son, you teach your son's son.
- A wise man hears only one word and understands two.
- It's true we have won all our wars, but we have paid for them. We don't want victories anymore.
- Don't be so humble; you are not that great.
- When President Nasser leaves instructions that he is to be awakened in the middle of the night if an Egyptian soldier is killed, there will be peace.
- Common sense is the collection of prejudices acquired by age eighteen.
- Any intelligent fool can make things bigger and more complex.
- It takes a touch of genius and a lot of courage to move in the opposite direction.
- Life is like riding a bicycle. To keep your balance, you must keep moving.
- When his wife asked him to change clothes to meet the German Ambassador, they want to see me, here I am. If they want to see my clothes, open my closet and show them my suits. – *Albert Einstein*
- I don't believe in mathematics. – *Albert Einstein*
- Intellectuals solve problems; geniuses prevent them. – *Albert Einstein*
- The hardest thing in the world to understand is income tax. – *Albert Einstein*
- You can't control the wind, but you can adjust your sails.
- The nice thing about being a celebrity is that if you bore people, they think it's their fault. – *Henry Kissinger*
- I don't want to become immortal through my work. I want to become immortal through not dying. - *Woody Allen*
- I'm not afraid of dying; I just don't want to be there when it happens! – *Woody Allen*
- Imagination is more important than knowledge. - (A sign hanging in *Einstein's* office at Princeton).

- Not everything that counts can be counted and not everything that can be counted counts. – *Albert Einstein*
- Education is what remains after one has forgotten everything he learned in school. – *Albert Einstein*
- Do not worry about your difficulties in Mathematics. I can assure you mine are still greater. – *Albert Einstein*
- Two things are infinite: the universe and human stupidity. And I'm not sure about the universe.
  - *Albert Einstein*
- I know not with what weapons World War III will be fought, but World War IV will be fought with sticks and stones. - *Albert Einstein*
- It has become appallingly obvious that our technology has exceeded our humanity. – *Albert Einstein*

SIGNS - SIGNS OF WHAT?

243

WHY AM I MARRIED?

- You have two choices in life: You can stay single and be miserable or get married and wish you were dead.
- At a cocktail party, one woman said to another, "Aren't you wearing your wedding ring on the wrong finger?" "Yes, I am. I married the wrong man."
- A lady inserted an ad in the classifieds: "Husband Wanted". The next day she received a hundred letters. They all said the same thing, "You can have mine."
- When a woman steals your husband, there is no better revenge than to let her keep him.
- A woman is incomplete until she is married. Then she is finished.
- A little boy asked his father, "Daddy, how much does it cost to get married?" The father replied, "I don't know son, I'm still paying."
- A young son asked, "Is it true Dad that in some parts of Africa a man doesn't know his wife until he marries her?" Dad replied, "That happens in every country, son."
- Then there was a woman who said, "I never knew what real happiness was until I got married, and by then, it was too late."
- Marriage is the triumph of imagination over intelligence.
- If you want your spouse to listen and pay strict attention to every word you say, talk in your sleep.
- Just think, if it weren't for marriage, men would go through life thinking they had no faults at all.
  - First guy says, "My wife's an angel!" Second guy remarks, "You're lucky, mine's still alive."
  - A woman's prayer: Dear Lord, I pray for Wisdom to understand a man, to Love and forgive him and for Patience for his moods. Because Lord, if I pray for Strength I'll just beat him to death."

AND NOW FOR THE FAVORITE!!!

A husband and wife are waiting at the bus stop with their nine children. A blind man joins them after a few minutes. When the bus arrives, they find it overloaded and only the wife and the nine kids are able to fit onto the bus. After a while, the husband gets irritated by the ticking of the stick of the blind man as he taps it on the sidewalk and says to him, "Why don't you put a piece of rubber at the end of your stick? That sound is driving me crazy." The blind man replies, "If you put a rubber at the end of YOUR stick, we'd be riding the bus, so shut the hell up!"

CARTOONS - A FRIEND IS LIKE A GOOD BRA #3

A friend is like a good bra: Hard to find, supportive, comfortable, always lifts you up, never lets you down or leaves you hanging and always close to your heart.

HORMONE HOSTAGE

The hormone hostage knows there are days in the month when all a man has to do is open his mouth and he takes his life into his own hands! This is a handy guide that should be as common as a driver's license in the wallet of every husband, boyfriend, co-worker or significant other.

Dangerous	Safer	Safest	Ultra Safe
What's for dinner?	Can I help you with dinner?	Where would you like to go for dinner?	Would you like some wine?
Are you wearing that?	Wow, you sure look good in brown.	WOW! Look at you!	Would you like some wine?
What are you so worked up about?	Could we be over reacting?	Here have my paycheck.	Would you like some wine?
Should you be eating that?	You know there are a lot of apples left.	Can I get you a piece of chocolate?	Would you like some wine?
What did you DO all day?	I hope you didn't over-do-it today?	I've always loved you in that robe!	Would you like some wine?

13 Things PMS stands for:

1. Pass my shotgun
2. Psychotic mood shift
3. Perpetual munching spree
4. Puffy mid-section
5. People make me sick
6. Provide me with sweets
7. Pardon my sobbing
8. Pimples may surface
9. Pass my sweat pants
10. Pissy mood syndrome
11. Plainly; men suck
12. Pack my stuff
13. Potential murder suspect

245

MATURE DRIVER

An older lady gets pulled over for speeding...

Older Woman: "Is there a problem, Officer"

Officer #1: "Ma'am, you were speeding."

Older Woman: "Oh, I see."

Officer: "Can I see your license please?"

Older Woman: "I'd give it to you but I don't have one."

Officer: "Don't have one?"

Older Woman: "Lost is, 4 years ago for drunk driving."

Officer: "I see. Can I see your vehicle registration papers please?"

Older Woman: "I can't do that."

Officer: "Why not?"

Older Woman: "I stole this car."

Officer: "Stole it?"

Older Woman: "Yes, and I killed and hacked up the owner."

Officer: "You what?"

Older Woman: "His body parts are in plastic bags in the trunk if you want to see."

The officer looks at the woman and slowly backs away to his car and calls for back up. Within minutes, 5 police cars circle the car. A senior officer slowly approaches the car, clasping his half drawn gun.

Officer #2: "Ma'am, could you step out of your vehicle please?"

The woman steps out of her vehicle.

Older Woman: "Is there a problem sir?"

Officer 2: "One of my officers told me that you have stolen this car and murdered the owner."

Older Woman: "Murdered the owner?"

Officer 2: "Yes, could you please open the trunk of your car?"

The woman opens the trunk, revealing nothing but an empty trunk.

Officer 2: "Is this your car ma'am?"

Older Woman: "Yes, here are the registration papers."

The officer is quite stunned.

Officer 2: "One of my officers claims that you do not have a driver's license."

The woman digs into her handbag, pulls out a clutch purse and hands it to the officer.

The officer examines the license. He looks quite puzzled.

Officer 2: "Thank you ma'am, one of my officers told me you didn't have a license, that you stole this car, and that you murdered and hacked up the owner."

Older Woman: "Bet the liar told you I was speeding, too." . . .

Don't mess with old ladies!!!

246

SLAP YOUR CO-WORKER DAY (THE HOLIDAY FOR WHICH WE HAVE ALL BEEN WAITING)

Tomorrow is the official **Slap Your Irritating Co-Workers Holiday:**

Do you have a co-worker who talks nonstop about nothing, working your last nerve with tedious and boring details that you don't care about?

Do you have a co-worker who ALWAYS screws up stuff creating MORE work for you?

Do you have a co-worker who kisses so much booty; you can look in their mouth and see what your boss had for lunch?

Do you have a co-worker who is SOOO obnoxious, when he/she enters a room, everyone else clears it?

Well, on behalf of Ike Turner, I am so very, very glad to officially announce tomorrow as 'Slap Your Irritating Co-Worker Day'.

Here are the rules:

- You can only slap one person per hour – no more.
- You can slap the same person again if they irritate you again in the same day.
- You are allowed to hold someone down as other co-workers take their turns slapping the irritant.

* No weapons are allowed; other than going upside somebody's head with a stapler or a hole-puncher.

* If questioned by a supervisor (or police), if the supervisor is the irritant, you are allowed to Lie, Lie, LIE!!!

Now, study the rules, break out your list of folks that you want to slap the living-day-lights out of and get to slapping!!!

CARTOONS - Dear Santa, If you leave a new bike under the tree, I will give you the antidote to the poison I put in the milk. Timmy

BARTENDER PSYCHOLOGY

Before you order a drink in public you should read this. Seven New York City bartenders were asked if they could nail a woman's personality based on what she drinks. Though interviewed separately, they concurred on almost all counts.

Ladies Drink Personalities:

Drink: Beer
Personality: Casual, low-maintenance and down to earth.
Your Approach: Challenge her to a game of pool.

Drink: Blender Drinks
Personality: Flaky, whiny, annoying; a pain in the ass.
Your Approach: Avoid her unless you want to be her cabana boy.

Drink: Mixed Drinks
Personality: Older, more refined, high-maintenance has very picky taste; knows EXACTLY what she wants.
Your Approach: You won't have to approach her. If she's interested, she'll send YOU a drink...

248

Drink: Wine (does not include White Zinfandel)
Personality: Conservative and classy;
sophisticated yet giggles.
Your Approach: Tell her you love to travel and   spend
quiet evenings with friends.

Drink: White Zinfandel
Personality: Easy; thinks she is classy and sophisticated, actually, she
has NO clue.
Your Approach: Make her feel smarter than she is...this should be an
easy target.

Drink: Shots
Personality: Likes to   hang with frat-boy pals and
looking to get totally   drunk...and naked.
Your Approach: Easiest hit in the joint. You
have been blessed.   Nothing to do but wait,
however, be careful not   to make her mad!

Drink: Tequila
No explanations required...everyone just KNOWS what happens there!

_____

THEN, there is the MALE addendum:
The deal with guys is, as always, very simple and clear cut:

Domestic Beer: He's poor and wants to **get laid**.
Imported Beer: He likes good beer and wants to **get**   **laid**.

Wine: He's hoping that the wine will give him a sophisticated image to
help him **get laid**.

Whiskey: He doesn't give a damn about anything but **getting laid**.

Tequila: He   is thinking he has a chance with the toothless
waitress.

White   Zinfandel: **He's gay.**

249

MAN AND HIS DOG

A man and his dog were walking along a road. The man was enjoying the scenery when it suddenly occurred to him that he was dead. He remembered dying and that the dog walking beside him had been dead for years. He wondered where the road was leading them. After a while, they came to a high, white stone wall along one side of the road. It looked like fine marble. At the top of the long hill it was broken by a tall arch that glowed in the sunlight. When he was standing before it, he saw a magnificent gate in the arch that looked like mother-of-pearl and the street that led to the gate looked like pure gold. He and the dog walked toward the gate and as he got closer, he saw a man at the desk to one side.

When he was close enough, he called out, "Excuse me, but where are we?" "This is Heaven, sir," the man answered. "Wow! Would you happen to have some water?" the man asked. "Of course, sir, come right in and I'll have some water brought right up." The man gestured and the gate began to open. "Can my friend," gesturing toward his dog, "come in, too?" the traveler asked. "I'm sorry sir, but we don't accept pets." The man thought a moment and then turned back toward the road and continued the way he had been going with his dog.

After another long walk and at the top of another long hill, he came to a dirt road leading through a farm gate that looked as if it had never been closed. There was no fence. As he approached the gate he saw a man inside leaning against a tree and reading a book. "Excuse me!" he called to the man. "Do you have any water?" "Yeah, sure, there's a pump over there, come on in." "How about my friend here?" the traveler gestured to the dog. "There should be a bowl by the pump." They went through the gate and sure enough, there was an old-fashioned hand pump with a bowl beside it. The traveler filled the water bowl and took a long drink himself, then he gave some to the dog.

When they were full, he and the dog walked back toward the man who was standing by the tree. "What do you call this place?" "This is Heaven," he answered. "Well, that's confusing," the traveler said. "The man down the road said that was Heaven, too." "Oh, you mean the place with the gold street and the pearly gates? Nope. That's Hell." "Doesn't it make you mad for them to use your name like that?" **"No, we're just happy they screen out the folks who would leave their best friends behind."**

OFFENSIVE JOKES - The Best for Last!

What do you call two Mexicans playing Basketball?
Juan on Juan

What is a Yankee?
The same as a quickie, but a guy can do it alone.

What is the difference between a Harley and a Hoover?
The position of the dirt bag.

Why is divorce so expensive?
Because it's worth it.

Why is air a lot like sex?
Because it's no big deal unless you're not getting any.

What do you call a smart blonde?
A golden retriever.

What do attorneys use for birth control?
Their personalities.

What's the difference between a girlfriend and a wife?
10 years and 45 lbs.

What's the difference between a boyfriend and a husband?
45 minutes.

What's black & white lying on the bed and crying?
A pregnant Nun.

What's black and white rolling on the bed and laughing?
The Priest that did it.

OFFENSIVE JOKES - The Best for Last!

What's the fastest way to a man's heart?
Through his chest with a sharp knife.

Why do men want to marry virgins?
They can't stand criticism.

Why is it so hard for women to find men that are sensitive, caring and good-looking? Because those men already have boyfriends.

What's the difference between a new husband and a new dog?
After a year the dog is still excited to see you.

Why do men chase women they have no intention of marrying? The same urge that makes dogs chase cars they have no intention of driving.

Why don't bunnies make noise when they have sex?
Because they have cotton balls.

What's the difference between a porcupine and a BMW?
A porcupine has the pricks on the outside.

What did the blonde say when she found out she was pregnant?
"Are you sure it's mine?"

Why does Mike Tyson cry during sex?
Mace will do that to you.

Why did OJ Simpson want to move to West Virginia?
Everyone has the same DNA.

OFFENSIVE JOKES - The Best for Last!

Why do drivers' education classes in Redneck schools use the car only on Mondays, Wednesdays and Fridays? Because on Tuesdays and Thursdays the Sex Ed class uses it.

Where does an Irish family go on vacation?
To a different bar.

Did you hear about the Chinese couple that had a blonde baby?
They named him 'Sum Ting Wong'.

What would you call it when an Italian has one arm shorter than the other?
A speech impediment.

What's the difference between a southern zoo and a northern zoo?
A southern zoo has a description of the animal on the front of the cage along with 'a recipe'.

How do you get a sweet 80 year old lady to say the 'F' word?
Get another sweet little 80 year old lady to yell 'BINGO'.

What's the difference between a northern fairytale and a southern fairytale?
A northern fairytale begins with "Once upon a time" and a southern fairytale begins "Y'all ain't gonna believe this . . ."

Why is there no Disneyland in Japan?
No one's tall enough to go on the good rides.

Why do men find it difficult to make eye contact?
Breasts don't have eyes.

(Congratulations, Gwen... Congratulations, Billie Jo) !

THANK YOU

for buying our book . . .

Billie Jo and Gwen

THE END

(Billie Jo, this is really cool !!! ga)

INDEX

258

259